Impact in Doctoral Educa

"This book connects impact and doctoral research, a crucial relationship in the era of accountable impact and engagement. It offers readers a panoramic insight into the doctoral research experience from multiple perspectives and showcases the diversity in doctoral journeys. The book offers excellent value to individuals embarking on a transformative learning journey. It provides insights into how the doctoral process is organized, the impact it can have on personal development both during and after the journey, as well as the academic and societal value of the end product, the doctoral thesis. Additionally, new leaders of doctoral programmes can benefit from the book as it offers valuable insights into key organizational dimensions of such programmes."

Wilfred Mijnhardt, *Policy Director at RSM Rotterdam School of Management, Erasmus University, Netherlands.*

Demonstrating how impact can be created and derived from doctoral programmes, this book focuses on their influence on academic knowledge, policy and practice. Significantly, it highlights the crucial impact of these programmes on the individual and the enduring consequences of this.

Drawing on their extensive experience and conversations with stakeholders in doctoral education from around the world, and incorporating real case examples, the authors provide practical guidance throughout the book which enables readers to enhance the design of new and existing doctoral programmes for greater impact. Each chapter ends with questions to stimulate reflection on the readers' experience of impact from doctoral education. The concluding chapter outlines a manifesto for enhancing and ensuring impact from doctoral research in the future.

With insights into the impact of doctoral programmes on individual researchers, this book will be essential reading for scholars of management education, as well as being a valuable resource for Higher Education administrators and senior academics around the world tasked with increasing impact from their doctoral programmes.

Emma Parry is Professor of Human Resource Management and Head of the Changing World of Work Group at the School of Management, Cranfield University, Bedfordshire, UK.

Colin Pilbeam is Professor of Organizational Safety at Cranfield University, Bedfordshire, UK.

BRITISH ACADEMY OF MANAGEMENT

Management Impact
Series Editors: Jean M. Bartunek, Nic Beech and Cary Cooper

Scholarly research into business and management proliferates globally. Its impact into management practice can be difficult to monitor and measure. This series, published in association with The British Academy of Management, presents Shortform books that demonstrate how management scholarship has impacted upon the real world.

Incorporating case study examples and highlighting the link between scholarship, policy and practice, the series provides an essential resource for postgraduate students and researchers seeking to understand how to create impact through their work. The concise nature of the books also ensures that they can be useful reading for reflective practitioners.

Delivering Impact in Management Research
When Does it Really Happen?
Robert MacIntosh, Katy Mason, Nic Beech and Jean M. Bartunek

Impact and the Management Researcher
Usha C.V. Haley

The Research Impact Agenda
Navigating the Impact of Impact
Martyna Śliwa and Neil Kellard

Impact in Doctoral Education
Product, Person and Process
Emma Parry and Colin Pilbeam

For more information about this series, please visit: www.routledge.com/Management-Impact/book-series/IMPACTM

Impact in Doctoral Education

Product, Person and Process

Emma Parry and Colin Pilbeam

Routledge
Taylor & Francis Group

LONDON AND NEW YORK

First published 2024
by Routledge
4 Park Square, Milton Park, Abingdon, Oxon OX14 4RN

and by Routledge
605 Third Avenue, New York, NY 10158

Routledge is an imprint of the Taylor & Francis Group, an informa business

British Library Cataloguing-in-Publication Data
A catalogue record for this book is available from the British Library

ISBN: 9781032378060 (hbk)
ISBN: 9781032378077 (pbk)
ISBN: 9781003342014 (ebk)

DOI: 10.4324/9781003342014

Typeset in Times New Roman
by codeMantra

Contents

Acknowledgements

The authors of this text had the privileged opportunity both to lead the doctoral programmes at Cranfield School of Management for several years and to teach, supervise and work with PhD and DBA students, and their supervisors and programme directors, not only at Cranfield but also at other universities in the UK, Europe and North America. This book is the result of the insights gained from that experience. We would therefore like to thank all of these colleagues and students for everything they have taught us over the last two decades.

We would also like to express our thanks to the following people for agreeing to a conversation in which they freely shared their insights and pointed us in interesting directions as part of our preparation for writing this book: Marko Bastl, Claire Collins, Tracy Davies, Owen Gower, Louis Grabowski, Alexander Hasgall, George Iliev, Carlos Mena, Wilfred Mijnhardt, Mark Saunders and Lucy Thorne. We have also drawn on earlier interviews with 30 graduates of the Cranfield Executive DBA programme. Thank you for providing such fantastic illustrations of the impact that one doctoral programme can have.

About the authors

Emma Parry is Professor of Human Resource Management and Head of the Changing World of Work Group at Cranfield School of Management. Emma has a long track record of leading doctoral programmes and working with a doctoral students and supervisors. She was previously President of the Executive DBA Council and a member of the European Foundation for Management Development (EFMD) Doctoral Programmes Committee and has worked with the British Academy of Management (BAM), the Chartered Association of Business Schools and the Association of MBAs in providing support and development to doctoral students and faculty involved in doctoral programmes. She was previously Director of the DBA and then Director of Doctoral Programmes for Cranfield School of Management. Emma is currently the Chair of BAM and Coeditor in Chief for the *International Journal of Human Resource Management*.

Colin Pilbeam is Professor of Organizational Safety at Cranfield University. He holds doctorates in both natural and social sciences and, so far, has supervised 18 doctoral students (both PhD and DBA) to successful completion. Previously, he was Director of the PhD programme at Cranfield School of Management and has worked with the European Institute for Advanced Studies in Management (EIASM) and the Economic and Social Research Council's (ESRC's) Advanced Institute of Management Research (AIM) to provide support and development opportunities for faculty involved in leading doctoral programmes. He has also delivered research training for doctoral students through the British Academy of Management (BAM) and also separately to universities in the UK and Europe. He has presented keynote addresses on doctoral education at the UK Council for Graduate Education (UKCGE) and European University Association–Council for Doctoral Education (EUA-CDE) annual conferences and published on this topic in *Studies in Higher Education*. He was Vice-Chair for Special Interest Groups in BAM in 2018–2019.

1 Introduction

Introduction

Over the past 20 years we have seen both the growth and diversification of doctoral programmes. In the UK alone, we saw over 113,000 people register for research degrees in 2021/2022 (104,645 at a doctoral level), with over 7,000 (7,150) choosing to focus on some area of Business and Management (HESA, 2023). A search for available doctoral programmes unearths 85 UK Business and Management PhD programmes (www.phdportal.com) and 52 Doctor of Business Administration (DBA) programmes (www.postgraduateresearch.com), from a total of around 160 UK universities. This means that the UK is potentially seeing a proliferation of doctoral graduates in Business and Management. In the UK, this picture is occurring against the backdrop of thriving Business and Management education in general: this subject group not only has the most students across UK higher education (one in six undergraduate and one in five postgraduate students are enrolled in a Business and Management subject), but it is also the most international, with 28% of the student population being from outside the UK (British Academy, 2021). The picture is similar elsewhere in the world, with the number and variety of Business and Management doctorates and doctoral graduates increasing.

Given this situation, it is perhaps surprising that more is not understood about the impact of doctoral programmes outside the qualifications that are awarded. While the notion of "impact" has been much discussed in higher education in recent years, particularly in relation to the value of academic research for beneficiaries outside academia, we are missing any detailed consideration of the role of doctoral research or doctoral researchers (Halse & Mowbray, 2011). Without this consideration, we might ask "what is the point of a doctorate?" particularly in Business and Management (or other Social Science fields) where the advances in knowledge might be less clear than in Physical Science subjects. This book therefore addresses the question: what is the impact of doctoral programmes? Building on other texts in this series (see, e.g., MacIntosh et al., 2021), we seek to examine the impact that doctoral programmes have at a variety of levels. In doing so, we contribute to the wider discussion on the relevance of Business and Management research

DOI: 10.4324/9781003342014-1

(e.g., Bartunek & Rynes, 2014). Doctoral programmes are particularly important in this discussion as they often represent the beginning of an individual's research journey and can therefore set the pattern and nature of this journey and the research that is conducted. Failure to consider relevance and impact at the outset is likely to drive future research that is equally lacking in these elements.

The nature of impact

To consider the impact of doctoral programmes, it is first important for us to understand what we mean by impact. MacIntosh et al. (2021: 3) define impact as "evidenced change occurring as a result of the purposeful application of co-developed knowledge". For us, the important aspect of this definition is the focus on *change* – for research to have real impact, it must lead to some kind of *change* that can be evidenced. A crucial question here is "impact on what?", "what will change as a result of the research?". Here we find useful the definition from the Economic and Social Research Council (ESRC, 2023) that divides impact into *academic impact* in which research leads to "shifting understanding and advancing scientific method theory and application" and *economic and societal impact* as the contribution that research can make to "… society and the economy and its benefits to individuals, organisations or nations". In the case of Business and Management research, we would argue that the latter of these two types of impact most commonly influences practice (whereby business and management practice is changed) or policy (where policy relating to business and management is changed). The ESRC develop these ideas through their distinction between *instrumental*, *conceptual* and *capacity building* forms of impact, suggesting that research can have impact, first, by shaping the development of policy, practice or services, shaping legislation and changing behaviour (*instrumental impact*); secondly, by contributing to understanding of policy issues and reframing debates (*conceptual impact*) or thirdly, through technical and skill development (*capacity building impact*).

A related question might ask "who does the research have impact on?". Any consideration of research impact must include the identification of the beneficiaries, stakeholders or end users of the research. This distinction highlights that impact can occur at a number of different levels – individual, organisational or societal – a distinction that is important to our discussions of doctoral programmes in this text. A final question relating to the nature of impact might be "is this impact always positive?". Certainly, the assumption in much of the discussions around research impact is that this involves change for the *better*. We reflect here on whether this is always the case in relation to doctoral programmes, or whether there are situations in which doctoral research or doctoral programmes might also have a negative outcome.

The context for research evaluation and impact

Research impact, including that from doctoral research, does not happen in a vacuum so it is important here to consider the context in which such impact plays out. While this book will discuss in some depth the characteristics of doctoral programmes and the structures, content and support mechanisms that might influence the impact of such programmes, the broader institutional and sector context also plays a role. With this in mind, we will focus mainly here on the UK context, drawing on comparisons with other countries as appropriate.

The notion of impact, outside scholarly impact, has become increasingly important within Business and Management academia globally. Indeed, successive presidents of the Academy of Management have raised concerns about the lack of practical impact of business and management research, with, for example, Don Hambrick as far back as 1994 asking, "*What if the Academy actually mattered?*" (Hambrick, 1994). These concerns are symptomatic of an ongoing debate within the Business and Management academia regarding the importance of rigour (scholarly quality) versus relevance (to stakeholders outside academia) (see for example MacIntosh et al., 2021; Pettigrew, 1997) and about the academic-practitioner gap conceptualised as the "*differing logics, time dimensions, communication styles rigor, and relevance and interests and incentives*" of the different parties (Bartunek & Rynes, 2014: 1181). A significant discussion in both academia and practice has focused on the idea of "evidence-based management" (see for example Briner et al., 2009) whereby managers draw on evidence as a basis for their decisions.

Alongside these global discussions, the emphasis in the UK research and Higher Education sector has also shifted to one with a greater emphasis on impact outside that with a scholarly focus. This can be demonstrated through a reflection on how research evaluation in the UK has changed over the past 20 years. This shift in context is perhaps most notably illustrated through three developments. Firstly, the change in research evaluation to include a greater emphasis on practical and societal impact over and above scholarly outputs. The replacement of the UK's Research Assessment Exercise (RAE) with the Research Excellence Framework (REF) in 2014 brought with it the requirement for institutions to submit impact case studies (representing 20% of the entire assessment) as a means of evaluating the impact of academic research outside academia. This emphasis on impact in research evaluation has grown since this time through the recommendation of the Stern report (2016) to deepen and broaden the notion of impact and the increase of the role of impact case studies from 20% to 25% in the 2021 REF process. Secondly, the move by many UK research funders (including the ESRC) to require funding applicants to develop a plan for achieving "pathways to impact" as part of the evaluation process. These two changes in the UK research landscape have driven higher education institutions to take the time to consider impact as a key part of research process and outcomes. Similar policy advances have occurred in other countries, such as the inclusion of research impact as part of the Excellence in Research for Australia (ERA) process. At an international level, a third initiative – the development of the San Francisco Declaration on Research Assessment (DORA) (https://sfdora.org/) – has put pressure on the sector to consider ways of evaluating research outputs outside traditional scholarly metrics such as journal rankings and citations. Taken together, these three elements reflect a context that is slowly recognising the importance of considering the broader practical and societal impact of academic research. This will inevitably be an important consideration for those directing doctoral programmes and those studying on them.

The nature of doctoral programmes

A doctorate is understood globally as the highest-level qualification available, typically achieved via the completion of some programme of research. Historically, the first doctoral degrees had an explicit professional orientation allowing scholars to participate fully in academia (Kot & Hendel, 2012), although in recent times the career selection of PhD graduates has been broader. Today, for the most part, a PhD consists of the production and defence of original research in the form of a doctoral thesis. The ESRC (2021a) describes three routes through a PhD programme in the UK: the traditional thesis-based route (taking three years full-time); a professional or practice-based route, where people undertake a PhD part-time alongside their job; and what ESRC call the "new" route which combines a one-year Masters in Research and a three-year research project (ESRC, 2021a). We would add to this a PhD by publications, in which an academic might take their existing publications and bring these together as a coherent body of research. We would also note the considerable variation within these models, with a plethora of different structures and content of both programmes and outputs. An important point of comparison here is that the UK PhD focuses primarily on the production of a research thesis rather than also passing interim qualifying exams as in the USA. While the "new" route is a slight variation of this structure with individuals expected to demonstrate their efficacy in a range of research methods before continuing to their own doctoral research, the UK PhD is still typically shorter than most overseas models such as those in the USA where people are expected to spend several years reaching proficiency in a subject before moving onto the research phase. In Europe, doctoral-level education was incorporated as the third cycle in the Bologna process in 2003. A subsequent seminar in Salzburg, Austria, in February 2005, developed a set of ten basic principles, which *inter alia* recognised the diversity of doctoral programmes in Europe but also that they should operate within an appropriate time duration, typically three to four years full-time (EUA, 2005).

Successful completion of a PhD is very much dependent on the notion of undertaking a rigorous programme of research to make a contribution to knowledge. The definition of what constitutes an academic contribution is much contested in the literature (see for example Whetten, 1989) but is often taken as referring to adding something new or novel to the subject area. By definition therefore, we could suggest the primary intended impact of a PhD may be in the academic or scholarly arena. A question that could be asked is; whether novelty in research findings is truly impactful? This will be considered later. It is often expected that a PhD will take the scholarly field forward in some way by building new theory or perhaps by challenging existing assumptions. What is not clear is how many PhDs truly have this level of impact in that they change something within their field, or whether we are conflating novelty with impact in this way when considering doctoral research.

A related question may be whether PhD research has impact outside the scholarly arena, for example, on practice or policy. Criticisms relating to the practice relevance of PhD research are cited as one reason behind the diversification of doctoral programmes, particularly in relation to the development of professional doctorates such as the DBA. Several authors have described the DBA as emerging in response to increasing demand for practice-relevant research (e.g., Banerjee & Morley, 2013). Indeed, professional doctorates in Business and Management (typically DBA programmes) are designed to produce knowledge which is practitioner-led and action-based (Bourner, 2016; Dos Santos & Fai Lo, 2018) and to make a scholarly contribution to practice with an equal but different kind of rigour (Banerjee & Morley, 2013; Neumann, 2005).

Rather than being seen as a means of developing future academics, the DBA is typically aimed at senior managers or professionals who want to learn and utilise research skills to benefit their career or their organisation or have a wider impact on policy and practice. The distinction between the PhD and the DBA is often described in that a traditional PhD develops *Professional Researchers*, where the DBA nurtures the *Researching Professional* (Bourner et al., 2001; Simpson & Sommer, 2016). Still typically research-based in the UK, the DBA differs from a full-time PhD also in structure being part-time and designed to enable individuals to undertake their doctoral research while working. The structure of DBA programmes will be discussed more in Chapter 7 of this book. Most notably, DBA research usually focuses on addressing a practical (or policy-led) problem and aims to provide useful outputs that can be directly utilised by relevant stakeholders. While some graduates of a DBA might decide to enter academia, more commonly they will remain in their current careers, therefore applying their research (and other) skills within an industry setting. Thus, it can be seen that the motivations and career outcomes of DBA students might differ significantly from PhD students.

The purpose and outputs of doctoral education

When considering the purpose and outputs of doctoral education, we can focus on two aspects, regardless of the type of doctorate. Firstly, the doctoral research or thesis which is commonly recognised as the deliverable from doctoral studies. The thesis is usually the basis of any defence or oral examination (*viva voce*) and stands as a record of the research that was done and its contribution to knowledge. We can think of the thesis as the *product* of the PhD or DBA studies. A second, and arguably more important, output of doctoral studies is the *person* who has undertaken the research – the doctoral graduate. An individual who has successfully completed a high-quality doctorate might exit their programme with a new set of skills, expertise and even mindset as a result of the learning and experiences that they have undertaken. In our opinion, the person is too often neglected when considering the outcomes – or impact – of doctoral study. Therefore, in this book we will focus on impact at the individual level as well as at the level of the organisation, sector or society.

The PhD and DBA, as the two dominant models of Business and Management doctoral programmes, clearly differ in purpose. This is important when considering their impact in relation to *product* or *person* and leads us to our next question: what should the purpose of doctoral education be? (and therefore, what impact *should* it have?). Taken at face value, the traditional PhD could be said to focus on developing scholarly research (*product*) and on preparing individuals for an academic career (*person*). Alternatively, the DBA aims to produce a *product* with practical relevance and useable outputs and to develop a *person* who can apply research skills within their practical career. Some, however, have questioned whether these ambitions are sufficient for doctoral research. Kirchherr (2018), for example, questions whether scholars generally (including doctoral students) should be aiming to improve society and therefore focus on producing useful outputs that can have real social impact. Questions that we will address in this book are whether doctoral programmes live up to these espoused and broader objectives? How can doctoral programmes better develop a product and person to achieve both scholarly and societal impact? In a context in which we are reminded regularly of the UN's sustainable development goals (SDGs) and in which our institutions commit to initiatives such as the Principles for Responsible Management Education (PRME) (https://www.unprme.org/), how can we create doctoral programmes that move beyond research that is designed to be published in the best journals and attract high numbers of academic citations but be actually used by nobody?. This takes us to the third "P" alongside *Product* and *Person* – that of the *Process* of doctoral programmes. Should we be designing programmes that will result in products and people for the good of society? How can we develop doctorates that genuinely produce research and graduates that will impact society for the better? These are big questions that, while we cannot promise to find answers, we will reflect on during the course of this text.

Purpose and structure of this book

Ultimately, the purpose of this book is to examine the impact of doctoral programmes. In doing so, we aim to broaden our understanding of the ways in which a doctoral programme might have impact – through the *product, person* and *process* – on individuals, organisations and society. To help us with this, we had conversations with academic colleagues in the USA and Europe (including the UK), and with senior colleagues in professional bodies and ESRC, before we commenced writing. We are grateful for their inputs. In the remainder of this book, we will explore the different types of impact that doctoral education might have: firstly, on scholarly knowledge (Chapter 2) and on policy and practice (Chapter 3); then on an individual's employability and career (Chapter 4) and on their deeper identity (Chapter 5). In our consideration of process, we will devote a chapter to the role of the supervisor and supervision (Chapter 6) because of their important influence before reflecting on the design of doctoral programmes (Chapter 7) and how this might facilitate different types of impact. Throughout our discussions, we would encourage readers to reflect on the true nature of the impact of doctoral programmes, whether this is always positive and how the sector and institutional context might influence this. As an aid to your reflection, we will provide some "points to ponder" at the end of each chapter.

Points to ponder

1 Do you recognise the distinction between instrumental, conceptual and capacity building impact of doctoral programmes? Or are there other forms of impact?
2 In your experience how do PhD and DBA programmes differ in their impact?
3 Why is the impact on the person neglected in current doctoral programmes?

Section 1

Product

2 Scholarly impact of doctoral research

Introduction

Successful doctoral students, according to the Quality Assurance Agency for Higher Education (QAA), UK, are those who have made a contribution through original research that extends the frontier of knowledge by developing a substantial body of work, some of which merits publication (QAA, 2014). Making a contribution to knowledge, and perhaps publishing these contributions, is therefore integral to the doctorate. But is either of these the same as scholarly impact, the subject of this chapter? Moreover, how do these evaluative criteria that are essential to achieving a doctoral qualification relate to each other or to the notion of impact?

For the doctoral student, a contribution to knowledge is captured characteristically in the thesis or *product*. Historically this was in the form of a monograph, but more recently, and particularly outside the UK, this may also take the form of a portfolio of papers or journal publications with an accompanying synopsis. The process of publication either as a book or as academic papers following peer review ratifies further the claim of contribution to knowledge recognised by the examiners in the award of the doctoral degree. Nevertheless, the question remains: is this scholarly impact?

This chapter focuses on four themes pertinent to a consideration of the scholarly impact of this product:

i   The definition of scholarly impact,
ii   The challenge of evaluating scholarly impact,
iii   The necessary foundations of scholarly impact, and
iv   The value of scholarly impact and for whom.

What constitutes scholarly impact?

Scholarly impact is an elusive term to define. Although the general notion may be understood and widely acknowledged as being important, its meaning in any specific context is indeterminate, and open to negotiation and appeal. The

DOI: 10.4324/9781003342014-3

phrase does, however, suggest that an identifiable domain of knowledge has been altered to a greater, or lesser, extent through some scholarly activity – in this case the research undertaken during the course of the doctorate. Drawing on our definition of impact as relating to change, this might therefore relate to change and development in the scholarly sense. Necessarily this change should be discernible by others, and ideally by many working in the same knowledge domain, or even beyond. In the context of a doctoral degree in Business and Management, this change is identified initially through the submission and assessment of a thesis by a small number of examiners. In the majority of cases, this is the limit of the scholarly impact of the thesis, which may be favourably described as weak in relation to its reach and significance.

Some doctoral research is published with the potential to reach a wider audience and shape the thinking and activity of other researchers. Often, this takes the form of academic journal articles, and these become a proxy measure for scholarly impact (IFSAM, 2021). The quality of journals in which research is published and the citations indicating that others are prepared to acknowledge the work (whether or not it has been read!) become key indicators. In Business and Management, unlike other disciplines, the decision of where to publish is constrained by journal rankings. While it is generally the case that those journals ranked highest on the list contain the best research, this is not necessarily so; journal rankings may be an unhelpful proxy for scholarly impact. However, as discussed in our last chapter, San Francisco Declaration on Research Assessment (DORA) aims to develop and promote best practice in the assessment of research and scholarly research. This global initiative may help to encourage a critical appraisal and assessment of the actual quality of an individual piece of work, rather than encouraging instant approval (or dismissal) based on the journal of publication. In the meantime, however, the hegemony of the journal list in Business and Management studies will prevail, at least in the background, shaping and constraining the style and format in which management knowledge is presented (IFSAM, 2021).

This conflation of scholarly impact with journal quality in Business and Management studies delimits the character of scholarly impact. Unlike some academic disciplines, Business and Management has a strong predilection for novelty, particularly theoretical novelty. Being able to establish the novelty of the contribution made by any piece of academic writing is critical for its successful publication, especially in those journals rated more highly (Miller, 2007). The exclusive pursuit of theoretical novelty further constrains the scope of scholarly impact. It precludes consideration of both atheoretical empirical studies which may illuminate new avenues of research that are consequential for a particular scholarly community and replication studies which can provide robust evidence to support practical interventions by managers in organisations (IFSAM, 2021). Broadening the scope of scholarly impact in Business and Management may be beneficial for not only academics but also doctoral researchers.

Currently, in most academic disciplines, scholarly impact is anchored in academic considerations of quality that are almost wholly focused on the written document (Denicolo & Park, 2013) or *product*. This is at the expense of other ways in which scholarly impact might be achieved, for example, through the development of highly educated individuals with the requisite skills to communicate with and educate others (the *person*). This after all was the original purpose of the doctorate to demonstrate adequate knowledge to permit the individual to teach others (Jones, 2018). In our current global higher education environment, this possibility is often downplayed, suggesting that the notion and meaning of scholarly impact has changed and perhaps narrowed over time, making it more difficult to achieve.

Yazdani and Shokooh (2018) challenge us to consider, amongst other things, the nature and characteristics of the *product* of doctoral-level study. A clearer and more broad-based definition than 'a contribution to knowledge which may merit publication' may allow us to appreciate the breadth of scholarly impact attainable through doctoral education in all of its many different formats currently available, without limiting it to an expression in a singular form.

How is scholarly impact in the doctorate evaluated?

The criteria for being awarded a doctorate typically refer to an original or novel contribution to knowledge. In the UK, the QAA advice on doctoral standards (QAA, 2014) provides the following descriptions of what is required for the award of a doctoral degree:

- The creation and interpretation of new knowledge, through original research or other advanced scholarship, of a quality to satisfy peer review, extend the forefront of the discipline and merit publication.
- A systematic acquisition and understanding of a substantial body of knowledge which is at the forefront of an academic discipline or area of professional practice.
- The general ability to conceptualise, design and implement a project for the generation of new knowledge, application or understanding at the forefront of the discipline, and to adjust the project design in the light of unforeseen problems.
- A detailed understanding of the applicable techniques for research and advanced academic enquiry.

Regulations at our own institution state more succinctly that the candidate's submitted work should contribute significant original knowledge, or the application of existing knowledge to new situations.

Both the general and the specific criteria emphasise originality, novelty and contribution (Baptista et al., 2015). However, the meanings of these criteria are somewhat ambiguous, especially in relation to scale and scope of the contribution to knowledge and the extent of originality. This leaves open the possibility of different local interpretations. While this may be advantageous in some circumstances, there is an underlying danger of a steady erosion of the standards required to meet the threshold of these criteria. Since examinations in the UK are closed and the *viva voce* is not a fully objective and impartial process but rather a socially constructed encounter (Park, 2005), this is entirely possible. The variability of this process, how the outcomes are decided and what influences this process will be considered more fully in Chapter 7. Notwithstanding these considerations, in our experience of doctoral examinations in the UK, the notion of scholarly impact is rarely assessed. Much more attention is given to the specification of the research question, the robustness of the execution of the methods, the clarification of findings and the implications for future research and sometimes practice. All of these are important and provide indications of the extent of the contribution to knowledge, but none directly addresses scholarly impact.

Wellington (2013: 1490) observes that "the notion of the doctorate varies across space, time and different disciplines", allowing others to question the appropriateness and sufficiency of these criteria and argue that they are too narrow to apply to the variety of doctoral degrees now on offer (Baptista et al., 2015). Searching for more appropriate criteria by which to examine a doctorate, Wellington examines the purpose, the impact, the regulations, the examination process and the voices of those involved in the examination. He concludes that each provides a partial answer and that the pursuit of Wittgenstein's notion of family resemblances may be more productive, because the search for the essential essence of a doctorate is futile. Others disagree. In the pursuit of describing common-to-all criteria for doctorates, Poole (2015) points to Trafford and Leshem's model of 'doctorateness' that synergistically combines 12 different elements, which should all be displayed in the written document, to a greater or lesser extent, to achieve a doctoral standard. Poole concludes by suggesting that some aspects of the thesis should be publishable, and that this criterion could be used, thereby "side-stepping the vexed issue of originality" (p. 1520).

An alternative to assessing scholarly impact through the outcome criteria of the *viva voce* is to assess the citations of the work in the medium term, assuming that it is published. However, not all doctoral research is published in peer-reviewed academic journals but remains relatively hidden in the thesis. Moreover, high citations counts may be achieved for reasons that are antithetical to scholarly impact. Anecdotally, literature reviews tend to receive more citations than empirical papers (regardless of quality), and a poor paper with a good definition of a construct may be cited purely for that definition. Focusing on citations emphasises the performance or productivity of research and tends to a narrow conceptualisation of the value of research, privileging its utility rather than its scholarship. Following this route, one is left wondering whether the doctorate has been hijacked to serve instrumental purposes, as Baptista et al. (2015) and Usher (2002) suggest, and the notion of scholarship jettisoned.

One of the challenges to identifying impact of any sort is defining the time-frame in which it is achieved or experienced. Exercises in ranking university research focus our attention on the more immediate time horizon. Individual career aspirations and the demands placed upon doctoral candidates seeking employment in universities require 'scholarly impact at pace'. Inevitably, this shapes the duration of doctoral programmes, and the nature of the research doctoral students pursue, favouring not only the investigation of more readily accessible problems, at the expense of those that are perhaps more important but less tractable, but also the analysis of quantitative data using statistical tools that is more readily published in a narrow range of academic journals.

All of this overlooks the possible benefits to be derived from 'blue skies' research at an indeterminate point in the future. While many doctoral theses languish in library repositories unread (and those that are read are seen only by other scholars), a prescient few will provide insights into problems and challenges that remain to be faced in the future. Our challenge is to remain aware of this potential resource.

The pursuit of scholarly impact also presumes that it can be predicted and planned. While this may be possible in some instances where known prob-lems are identifiable, serendipity is also an important feature of scholarly endeavour, and this often creates significant impact. This is unpredictable and unplanned but should be encouraged over the longer term offering the opportunity for paradigm shifts and the radical evolution of ideas. Scanning the editorials of leading journals in the field of Business and Management suggests that this is a rare occurrence, at best. Instead, the peer-review pro-cess of high-profile journals is conservative favouring 'gap-spotting' research (Ashkanasy, 2011).

Underpinnings of scholarly impact

Scholarly impact is supported by three key factors (training, supervision and funding), which we will briefly consider here but elaborate more fully in Chapters 6 and 7.

Firstly, training in research methods is essential if a doctoral student is to undertake a programme of research that will be sufficiently rigorous to deliver scholarly impact. The Economic and Social Research Council's (ESRC's) pe-riodic accreditation of doctoral programmes at UK universities to determine the award of studentships benefits students through the need for universities to provide a structured programme of training primarily in research methods. In more recent rounds, this has been augmented by training in transferable skills. Undoubtedly this helps to raise standards, but only for those fortunate to partic-ipate in the programme, and unfortunately this has sometimes been restricted only to those in receipt of an ESRC studentship, and not to others who may also have embarked on their PhD journey at the same time. The structure of such programmes may also preclude the attendance of students studying part-time or located at a distance from the campus. Nevertheless, without some grasp of the variety of research philosophies and methodologies that inform research in Business and Management, it is unlikely that doctoral students will successfully build upon existing work and make a scholarly contribution.

High-quality supervision where supervisors support students and engage with them in their research is a second key factor. Supervisors who themselves are unaware of the latest developments in their field of knowledge or self-constrained in their approach to research may stifle the creativity of the doctoral students studying with them. In the worst cases, this leads to simple replication studies of earlier work that are of limited value. Suggesting alternative lines of inquiry and the use of different theoretical perspectives, without being prescriptive, and the possible exploration of hitherto unnoticed connections that develop curiosity are important contributions that supervisors can make to the scholarly impact of doctoral student work. Supervision must also encompass the well-being of the student. The achievement of scholarly impact is unlikely from students who are unsupported pastorally.

A final key factor is funding. Without support students often withdraw (McAlpine & Norton, 2006). Students receiving financial support can devote themselves full-time to their studies for several years and are more likely to pursue research that is published allowing scholarly impact. Moreover, a funded research project to which a student is attached may already have an associated plan for achieving scholarly impact. An analysis of publications derived from funded research in Canada supports this argument. Larivière (2013) explored the relationship between scholarship, productivity, impact and completion for more than 27,000 doctoral students from the province of Quebec, Canada, between 2000 and 2007, and found funded students published more than unfunded students. Students in Business and Management were, however, an exception to this rule. His analysis showed that the published work of unfunded, part-time, PhD students had more citations than that from funded students. Although no reasons for this are given, we suggest that this may be because unfunded part-time students, perhaps, have a greater appreciation of the challenges of practising managers and policymakers so their research is more topical. They may also have access to data that others, who are removed from the workplace, do not, which makes their publications more appealing.

Place of scholarly impact – who values it?

New ideas are an essential foundation for a knowledge economy. Governments in the West have placed research and development at the heart of their economic policies (Lambert, 2003; Sainsbury, 2007), anticipating that the effective and efficient management of knowledge, as a factor of production (Usher, 2002), will lead to continued economic prosperity. Acting as an engine of new ideas to produce knowledge, doctoral research is positioned to make a significant contribution (Pedersen, 2014). Evidence to support, or refute, the extent of this contribution is unavailable, but anecdotal observation would suggest that the impact of doctoral research in Business and Management studies on the wider economy of most countries is limited at best. Part of the explanation for this underwhelming contribution may result from the diversity of stakeholders who have an interest in scholarly impact and who consequently frame its definition to suit their purposes. These may conflict, diluting the overall perception of impact. The following briefly describes some of these different purposes.

For those doctoral researchers, typically full-time PhD students, seeking an academic career, attaining recognition for their scholarship through successful publications in higher quality journals is a matter of high priority. Recruitment to lectureships or postdoctoral research positions is influenced strongly by a record of publications or submission-ready articles. For those wishing to pursue a career outside academia, including Doctor of Business Administration (DBA) or part-time PhD students already employed in organisations, this is less important. For these individuals scholarly impact can be more broadly defined.

Supervisors too may also seek to benefit from the publications prepared by their students. However, their purposes may be broader. Supervising doctoral students permits academic staff to expand their domain of focus, for example, by pursuing interesting and potentially fruitful avenues that have commended themselves from prior work, or by deploying new methods to existing research areas to create new data sets or provide fresh insights. A survey conducted in 2021 of doctoral supervisors in UK Higher Education Institutions reported that 82% of respondents agreed that "being a research supervisor improves the quality of my own research" (UKCGE, 2021). In these situations, scholarly impact may legitimately refer to the professional development of existing academics.

Higher education institutions may place a different emphasis on scholarly impact. The manifestation of scholarly impact in publications is essential for submission to sector-wide national assessments of research quality. In the UK, recurrent funding from government is allocated to each university in proportion to the volume of its published research identified as being of the highest quality according to the criteria of originality, significance and rigour (HEFCE, 2019). These have come to define scholarly impact. Performance in this assessment affects reputation amongst key stakeholders and therefore income.

Other organisations, beyond the Higher Education sector, may have a different perspective on scholarly impact. In many cases, they are unaware of the new ideas or uncertain how to exploit the findings of this new knowledge in their particular circumstances. Assistance is necessary to interpret the findings and translate them into tangible products that have utility. Organisations are also sceptical of the potential contribution doctoral graduates can make to a workplace lacking knowledge of their distinctive competencies (McAlpine & Inouye, 2022).

Several studies (Couston & Pignatel, 2018; De Grande et al., 2014) have shown that organisations do not necessarily value the research skills and knowledge possessed by PhD graduates, and developed through their research training, preferring others, such as technical skills, communication, project management and teamwork, that are not necessarily developed explicitly during a research degree. We consider this further in Chapter 4. For these organisations, scholarly impact of either the *product* or the *person* is relatively unimportant.

While most Social Science students in the UK commence their doctoral studies aspiring to an academic or research career in universities, this changes during their studies in favour of careers beyond Higher Education, often in public or third sector organisations (ESRC, 2021a). A survey of UK domiciled PhD students showed that 3.5 years after graduation an overall majority of PhD holders had left academia, and only 50.6% holders of Social Science PhDs remained in academic employment (Hancock, 2021). Some authors argue that this contributes to the general upskilling of the national workforce through the positive interactions that occur between graduates and non-graduates in the workplace (Casey, 2009). While there may by specific instances of this, this ripple effect is likely to be limited and the effects slow to diffuse through the wider labour market. Others argue that more highly educated individuals contribute to the public good, creating a better society in which to live (East et al., 2014), and so scholarly impact is related to the improvement of wider society.

Conclusion

Reporting on PhD education in the USA at the start of the new millennium, Nyquist and Woodford (2000) noted that the PhD "is the pinnacle of academic accomplishment, whose recipients offer so much to the knowledge society of the 21st Century". The foregoing discussion suggests that the scholarly contribution to knowledge of doctoral research may not realise the potential implied by Nyquist and Woodford. This view was supported by some of the senior academics we interviewed for the book. The contribution to knowledge of more recent graduates who are encouraged to simply replicate prior studies is often weak, and any scholarly impact is absent. It is perhaps in other areas that doctoral researchers make their impact. Mowbray and Halse (2010: 654) note that in Australia a dominant discourse of the PhD is "the timely production of a marketable product – the skilled PhD graduate". It is to these alternative, more obviously utilitarian and practical contributions that we now turn.

Points to ponder

1 What changes to doctoral education would be required to enable scholarly impact?
2 What are the strengths and weaknesses of the different definitions of scholarly impact?

3 Practitioner and policy impact of doctoral research

Introduction

Research in Business and Management has set itself the 'double hurdle' of being both rigorous and relevant (Pettigrew, 1997) with the intention of achieving positive impact on the performance of organisations through rigorous investigation. Alongside this, as discussed in Chapter 1, practitioners and managers are aiming to be more evidence-based in their approaches to decision-making which should encourage practical application of research. Professional doctorates, in their course specifications and intended learning outcomes (ILOs), often emphasise the importance of the practical application of the research that will be conducted. For example, Georgia State University claims in relation to their Executive Doctor of Business Administration (DBA) that "*upon graduation, you will be able to apply research methodology and business theory to practical problems, and develop new perspectives on leadership, global change, and decision making*".[1] Aston Business School in the UK claims that their DBA helps executives to "*leverage their professional experience with cutting edge research-based skills*".[2] More broadly, the website of the Executive DBA Council (EDBAC) describes a DBA as focusing "*on topics at the intersection of theory and contemporary business issues*".[3] This focus is less noticeable in traditional doctorates. In some respects, therefore, the professional doctorate rather than the PhD more fully aspires to the dual standards of research espoused by Business and Management studies. In cases where the doctoral research is rigorously performed, professional doctorates do have noticeable impact (see the illustrations in Boxes 1–5). Unfortunately, there is a wide variation between universities in the standards achieved by professional doctorates. Rigour is not always assured, and furthermore impact may be limited.

Acknowledging this need for practical relevance and impact on organisations and policy, this chapter explores the nature of this impact and the forms it takes, before considering how impact generated through doctoral research can be evaluated and some of the challenges associated with this. The chapter also suggests ways in which the achievement of impact on policy and practice can be supported.

DOI: 10.4324/9781003342014-4

What constitutes impact on policy and practice?

While the route to scholarly impact through academic publications is commonly understood (see Chapter 2), the path to practitioner or policy impact is much less clear and comparatively less travelled, even though impact has become an established part of the Higher Education landscape, at least in the UK (Watermeyer & Hedgecoe, 2016). In part this is because historically engagement of academics with practice has not been extensively encouraged. In the UK, this was limited to those applying for UK Research and Innovation (UKRI) funding who are obliged to provide impact summaries and pathways to impact as part of the bidding process. The introduction of impact case studies, which describe specific examples of impacts achieved during the assessment period, into the UK's Research Excellence Framework (REF) in 2014 heightened the awareness of impact amongst a wider academic community. Nevertheless, a lack of engagement with practitioners and policymakers is often still the case. The primary focus of many academics is to publish in highly rated academic journals and, where necessary, teach on undergraduate and graduate programmes.

In addition, and perhaps more significantly, the nature of the *product* that generates practice or policy impact is poorly specified, being contingent frequently upon context. For example, it may take the form of a model or framework (Box 3.1). It may be a tool to enable organisational change (Box 3.2). Alternatively, it may provide an analysis that disrupts current thinking (Box 3.3). Interventions, such as these, potentially provide significant impact but are limited often to a single organisation. Greater impact can be achieved through developments at a national level either within a sector (Box 3.4) or in national government policies. Many of the more highly rated impact cases submitted to the UK's REF process have policy impact (Bastow et al., 2014) allowing them more easily to meet the criteria for evaluating impact of 'reach and significance' (HEFCE, 2019). However, establishing the link between research output and eventual policy development or change is both slow and difficult. Policy changes may take years before they are finally approved, and

---

Box 3.1   Enabling emergency healthcare

Concern over the quality of healthcare delivery is common in many countries. One study of physician perceptions of this provided a conceptual model that categorised perceptions of enablers and barriers to quality healthcare. This enabled change in the Norway's largest emergency hospital and triggered a debate in the Norwegian government about how hospital emergency care can best be provided nationally.

Box 3.2   'Fewer, Bigger, Better'

Reducing waste is an important feature of the sustainability agenda, especially in the footwear and apparel industry where 80% of products are replaced every six months. To avoid wasteful new product development, a DBA study developed the concept of feedforward anticipatory control (Baker & Bourne, 2014) and designed a tool for use by new product development teams to increase portfolio value and strategic alignment with compelling benefit. Total product range was reduced by a quarter and margin per product was increased by 50%.

Box 3.3   Uncovering retail customer preferences

DBA students, because of their seniority, often have unrivalled access to data that can be deployed to investigate phenomena that are conventionally studied in the laboratory. One of these is customer decision-making. An analysis of secondary data from more than 30,000 shoppers within a major supermarket chain demonstrated that to encourage spending stores should invest in personalised customer services and checkout customer services ahead of changes to in-store environment. This is counter to the current trend towards creating a clinical in-store environment and providing self-service checkouts.

Box 3.4   Avoiding bad debt

DBA studies may have potentially significant social impact. In some countries, companies provide loans to individuals to pay for their medical bills. The decision to loan money (or not) is driven by an algorithm, which in one company was shown by analysis to support decisions to make payments to those who would become bad debt, while discriminating against those who could make the repayments. Adjustment to the algorithm has resulted in the loan company having more money to lend to those capable of repaying the loan, and not drawing others into indebtedness. The change in this company spawned a change in other loan companies nationally.

often have multiple sources. The contribution of doctoral research is therefore more equivocal in these policy settings.

Besides a *product*, practitioner impact might also be achieved through the individual themselves. Armsby et al. (2018) noted that professional doctorates are vehicles for organisational change through the individuals studying for them. In some cases, this may be through an insight that reorients the perception of an individual. If they are sufficiently senior in their organisations, the consequences for the organisation and those working in it can be profound. A recent DBA graduate at Cranfield held a senior position with responsibility for talent management amongst managers in a large global pharmaceutical company. Initial discussions on a likely research topic focused on the managerial ambition to make improvements to the talent management programme. However, challenging the justice and fairness of others making selection decisions on who to allocate to a high potential development programme based on performance at a single point in time, suggested an alternative route. This exposed a much more mixed view of the merits of the talent management programmes with both 'high' and 'low' performers equally expressing antipathy and indifference, but occasionally, satisfaction with the process.

In other cases, the impact may arise from the transformational journey experienced by the individual researcher. They become the force for impact. Programmes of doctoral study that incorporate a strong reflective component facilitate this kind of personal transformation. At one UK business school, DBA students write both short chapters of influential periods of their life history and responses to set questions, which are shared in small, facilitated groups which meet regularly during their registration. These develop a deeper sense of self-awareness, and the personal impact is profound. Wellington (2013), commenting on the outcomes of an earlier study reviewing student perceptions of the impact of professional doctorates, noted that many of those narratives focused on the students' own personal development and growth rather than the development of the profession or professional knowledge, which is often an espoused aim of professional doctorates (ESRC, 2005). This is considered more fully in Chapter 5.

Separately from considerations of the form of the impact, it is important to recognise that Business and Management is not a singular subject; rather it is comprised of disciplines and specialities. Any discussion of impact ought to recognise this variation and acknowledge that sub-disciplines may have different types of impact that are achieved in different ways. Hughes et al. (2019) analysed impact case studies from UK REF2014 and reported differences between disciplines in whether they claimed policy or practice impact. Economics, for example, claimed a significantly lower proportion of practice impact than other disciplines, like Marketing. Operations Management and Organisation Studies claimed a very small proportion of policy impact but a very high proportion of practice impact. In all cases, claims for impact focused on the specific actions taken by practitioners or policymakers, rather than on quantifiable results, especially in Human Resource Management (HRM). Direct influence on the public was rare, although indirect influence was commonly claimed in Economics, HRM and Marketing. It might be appropriate therefore to anticipate different forms of impact from doctoral students studying in different disciplines within the broad field of Business and Management. Institutional practices to support impact delivery from doctoral studies may need to take account of this difference.

How and when is impact on policy and practice evaluated?

Unlike scholarly impact, the criteria for the evaluation of practitioner and policy impact are considerably less clear and not universally agreed (Watermeyer, 2016). In the UK, two criteria, namely reach and significance, have been used in the national assessment exercises (HEFCE, 2019). Some would argue that these are nonetheless limited and restrictive. Bandola-Gill and Smith (2022) conclude that only four plot lines were observable in the narratives of a sample of impact case studies submitted to the UK's REF exercise in 2014, namely problem-solving, tool building, reframing and public engagement. They also noted the essential linearity of the argument in these narratives and their emphasis on monetising the value of the impact. Together these "construct a very specific vision of impact" (p. 1868). They suggest that the standardisation of this format has come to define what impact means and they contrast 'REF impact' from meaningful research impact. It is noteworthy that the illustrations of DBA impact (see Boxes 1–5) conform to some of these plot lines. Perhaps professional doctorates too have succumbed to the institutional pressures to consider impact only in particular ways, preferring the 'fairy tale' versions of impact to the messy, complex and insufficiently persuasive narratives that characterise 'real' impact (Bandola-Gill & Smith, 2022).

The ambiguity and uncertainty surrounding the evaluation of practitioner and policy impact ensures that it is regularly overlooked in the examination of the doctoral thesis (Wellington, 2013), and most, if not all, of the assessment focuses on the academic aspects of the thesis. This is unfortunate, especially for those studying for the award of a professional doctorate, where practice or policy impact is one of the intended contributions. A key factor in this will be the selection only of examiners from academic institutions. Their capabilities and interests will necessarily focus away from practice and policy impact. We will consider further the selection of examiners in Chapter 7.

The only point at which the impact of a doctoral thesis will be formally assessed is at the oral examination. Evidently, this can only consider the extent of impact in the short term. Even in the most dynamic organisations this is likely to be limited, and so little can be said about impact in the examination discussion. Opportunities to identify continued further impact are not routinely available and so overlooked. Yet they may occur. Periodic follow-up interviews/conversations with the doctoral graduate might allow this information to be captured, but this takes more time and presumes an interest by both supervisor and student in monitoring the process, and moreover, a positive working relationship between them, which may not always be the case.

Policy and practice impact in the medium to long term often comes from those students who convert their experience of research training and the findings from their thesis into consultancy offerings. In our experience, these often form the basis of impact on a greater variety of organisations over a longer period (Box 3.5).

There is, however, a particular challenge with identifying practitioner impact, namely commercial sensitivities and the need for non-disclosure agreements (NDAs). In some cases, organisations, particularly larger commercial firms, only allow access for data collection if NDAs are signed. This prevents the wider communication of results and opportunities for improvement more widely. Inevitably, this hampers wider progress, which from a societal perspective makes little sense. It also prevents the more rapid differentiation between successful and unsuccessful ideas because companies can unknowingly fall into the same traps as others, making the same mistakes, which may have been prevented with a wider sharing of knowledge.

This suggests that there is little systematic or consistent assessment of the impact of doctoral research in Business and Management on policy or practice. In part this is because the criteria for evaluation are limited, demanding a formulaic presentation which may not always be appropriate. In addition, universities are oriented towards scholarly impact, and, even though DBA programmes are designed for practical impact, students experience this normative pressure, resulting in DBA theses that resemble those produced by

---

Box 3.5   From executive to consultant

Skills and knowledge acquired during doctoral studies can enable graduates to transition effectively and confidently to freelance roles, acting as consultant, coach, advisor, facilitator, mentor or researcher as required by organisations that purchase their services.

Building on a study of collaborative working, Peter now offers business and HR consulting and training specialising in collaborative leadership and working together within and between organisations. While Ruth's doctoral work sought to reconcile the tension between the objectives of planned change and prevailing organisational routines. She is now a 'recognised leader of project-based organisational change'.

PhD students with an emphasis on scholarly impact. We consider how DBA programmes can be designed to resist this pressure in Chapter 7.

Who values impact on policy and practice and why?

Practitioner impact, as we have noted, occurs in a variety of ways amongst diverse stakeholders. Moreover, discussion often focuses on utilitarian motives. For the key stakeholder, the research student, the motive is often different. Experience and curiosity combine to shape a problem that has to be explored. It is this personal interest that sustains enthusiasm and commitment, even during the most challenging of times. Many of our DBA students experience these during their studies, and still successfully complete their doctorates. For example, one of our DBA researchers who had experienced a long career in the public sector joined the programme frustrated at the failure of the public sector to manage performance effectively. This researcher focused her research on finding out why this was. Despite facing significant personal health problems which developed during the course of the programme, the researcher successfully graduated.

Motivations to supervise DBA students, and pursue practical impact, vary. While some supervisors are keen on making practical impact, others take on supervision of these students reluctantly seeing no potential for publication and scholarly impact; a view we do not share. Papers written by DBA students may be (and have been) as highly cited as others.

At an institutional level, motivations to recruit DBA students often centre on income generation potential rather than on achieving policy or practice impact through their work. Anecdotally, in some institutions, DBA programmes with their avowed practice orientation are seen as a 'cash cow' rather than being valued as a scholarly degree. Fees for professional doctorates are often higher than for PhD students, especially those also studying part-time.

In the UK, universities view policy and practice impact through the lens of REF, with a particular emphasis on developing impact case studies. Interest in the outputs from DBA students is limited to the extent that they satisfy REF requirements. However, this is problematic since case studies of single organisations (the typical focus of DBA inquiry) rarely have the necessary scope to satisfy the REF criteria of reach and significance and be rated highly. A broader case study is often required with multiple inputs, of which a DBA thesis may be one. Consequently, the specific effects of a single DBA thesis are often overlooked.

Contributions by universities to economic and societal benefits through policy and practice impact are expected increasingly by national governments in return for ongoing financial support to the Higher Education sector. In the UK, a series of policy reviews firmly established this 'impact turn' (Lambert,

2003; Sainsbury, 2007; Warry, 2006). UK government spending on science is kept under regular review, placing pressure on key stakeholders in the Higher Education sector to deliver tangible benefits to the economy and society. This broad scope, however, is rarely the focus of study for individual DBA students.

Impact on policy and practice is perceived differently by each of the stakeholders in doctoral education. For students, often DBAs, the interest genuinely lies in solving an important organisational problem. For the universities offering the research degree, the interest is more on the income the DBA students generate or the continued financial support from government arising from a carefully crafted narrative to convince peers of the impact of the research.

What supports the delivery of practitioner impact?

Successfully impacting practice or policy is contingent upon a number of factors. Some of these replicate those necessary for scholarly contributions (noted in Chapter 2), but not all. Moreover, even those that appear similar have a different nuance.

Two factors that are unique for policy and practice impact are appropriate selection of suitable candidates and the level of support they have from their organisation. Perhaps the easiest way to influence practice within organisations is for those engaged in the research project to be embedded in the organisation and have sufficient authority to initiate changes. Similarly, policy impact is more readily affected by those with direct connections to the policymaking processes, for example, through committee membership and industrial advisory groups. The selection, therefore, of students with experience of important organisational challenges and connections to other influential groups is an obvious and easy way to lay foundations that are likely to facilitate practice and policy impact. Some institutions make this an intentional part of their research strategy.

A second factor is the level of support the doctoral student receives from their organisation. Doctorates take several years to complete, and in such a timeframe a variety of circumstances can arise that potentially disrupt progress. For example, organisational strategies change, and markets grow or collapse, making resources to support the student vulnerable. Changes in personnel with different priorities can make access to data more challenging. Additionally, individuals may be made redundant, or made lucrative offers by other firms, so that there is no continuity in organisational context for data collection. These vagaries of the workplace, and others like them, render doctoral student research vulnerable to disruptions that can jeopardise the prospect of practice impact. Our experience is that part-time students frequently change roles or employers during their studies and managing this transition to minimise its impact on the coherence of the research project can be challenging for both the student and the supervisor.

The role of the supervisor is crucial at such times of transition. In addition to the necessary emotional and intellectual support that may be required, supervisors can also enable policy and practice impact through their own network of contacts. Access to senior experienced practitioners working in a particular area of interest provides fertile ground for new ideas. As Marcos and Denyer (2012) note, access to senior practitioners also provides up to date access to topical challenges faced by organisations and potential access for data collection to investigate the phenomenon. Finally, these practitioners provide a community to validate and critique the work, suggesting appropriate and accessible avenues for presentation and access to receptive audiences. These connections provide access to organisations for full-time students, who perhaps lack current direct access to relevant communities of practice.

Training is an essential part of any doctorate. Originally focussed on developing competence in research methods, it increasingly now incorporates a wider set of 'transferable skills', including project and budget management, ability to communicate with a broad range of audiences and collaborative working and multidisciplinary perspectives to problem-solving (ESRC, 2021a). This will be discussed in more detail in Chapter 4. While younger full-time doctoral students, with limited experience, may require training in transferable skills, such as team-working or communication to a variety of audiences, this may not be so for part-time students, who can be highly experienced. Their ability to negotiate (perhaps explaining why something has not been delivered!) and make presentations to groups is often of the highest quality. With this population of students, the greater challenge is to encourage and support the development of their research and writing skills. Often this can be resented. Successful individuals rarely take kindly to critical challenge, but inevitably this is what they experience when embarking on a doctorate. Managing their learning and supporting them through this developmental process is essential if the foundations for rigorous research are to be laid. Having developed their research capabilities, the possibilities for successful impact are heightened considerably (Boxes 3.2 and 3.5).

In addition to training in 'transferable skills', there is a family of approaches to research in Business and Management studies that enable the imbrication of knowledge from research and from practice (Sharma & Bansal, 2020). Training in these approaches may stimulate practice and policy impact. Systematic literature reviews, as part of evidence-based management, encourage the use of research evidence to support managerial decision-making (Briner et al., 2009). Design thinking anticipates close and continuous interaction between researchers and customers or other end users in the design, development and delivery of products and services (Liedtka, 2013). And proponents of Mode 2 knowledge production (Gibbons et al., 1994; Tranfield & Starkey, 1998) advocate a process of co-production of knowledge between researchers and practitioners in the context of application. The resulting knowledge products, or field-tested and grounded technological rules, solve complex and relevant field problems in a number of settings (van Aken, 2005).

A final distinctive contribution to practice impact is the availability of a variety of media for communicating the ideas widely. Practitioner-facing journals, such as *Harvard Business Review* (HBR) or *California Management Review* (CMR), offer opportunities to disseminate findings to a wider audience. Similarly, other professional and practice journals provide outlets to potentially receptive audiences in the particular field of work. Ranking less highly than HBR or CMR, and indeed scholarly journals more generally, these are often overlooked as ways to promote research findings to those who might use them. Increasingly, social media provide opportunities to communicate research in short snippets and encourage adoption.

Conclusion

Professional doctorates such as the DBA aim to enhance executive and professional practice, and by grappling with real and complex issues to transform businesses and organisations. While in general some claim that research in Business and Management studies has delivered this, as demonstrated through the impact studies submitted by UK universities to REF2014 (Pidd & Broadbent, 2015) or REF2021, others argue that the impact has been negative (Ghoshal, 2005). At a sector level, the aggregate impact of professional doctorates on policy and practice is unknown. In part this is because this is not a priority metric for universities offering the award. At an individual level, however, the impact is variable but may be huge. We shall consider this impact on the *person* further in the next section.

Points to ponder

1   How is practical or policy impact actually achieved? Through the product or the person?
2   What criteria might reasonably be deployed at the final examination to assess impact on practice?
3   To what extent has the definition of practice impact been constrained? How might you comprehensively define impact on practice?

Notes

1 https://robinson.gsu.edu/program/dba/.
2 https://www.aston.ac.uk/study/courses/executive-doctor-business-administration-dba-online.
3 https://edbac.org/degree.

Section 2

Person

4 Impact on individual skills, employability and career progression

Introduction

As described in Chapters 2 and 3, doctoral research may have a significant scholarly or practical impact on the external world. While the importance of these outcomes cannot be denied, seeking scholarly or practical impact are rarely the motivations that drive an individual to undertake doctoral study. Many doctoral researchers are driven, at least partly, by the anticipated impact of a doctoral qualification on their own career or employability, rather than a higher-level desire to achieve impact at an organisational, sector or societal level. Bryan and Guccione (2018) show that doctoral students commonly obtain value from doctoral study in four areas: career, skills, social and personal values. None relate directly to scholarly or practical impact.

Research confirms that the motivations of doctoral students are primarily related to either career-related aspects such as the desire for a professional or academic career or to obtain a job or employment (or be promoted to more senior employment) or self-improvement such as the development of subject-related knowledge or research skills (Brailsford, 2010; Wiegerová, 2016). So, for the individuals embarking on a doctoral programme at least, a large part of their focus may be on achieving impact at an individual level, specifically in relation to improved employability and career development, rather than on the impact on academic knowledge or practice. This section will therefore discuss the potential impact of doctoral programmes on the *person*. We start this discussion with a focus on an individual's skills, employability and career progression.

Individual and programme objectives in relation to employability and careers

Doctoral programmes are widely expected to have an impact on employability and career progression at an individual level (Diamond et al., 2014). A recent survey of PhD students (Cornell, 2020) found that the vast majority of PhD students believed that their doctorate would improve their employability.

DOI: 10.4324/9781003342014-6

However, it is also clear that this potential impact might differ according to the nature and content of the doctorate undertaken, according to the subject area focus and the institution attended. The impact of doctoral study on an individual's career and employability is also likely to depend, to some extent, on whether the doctorate undertaken is a traditional PhD programme or a professional doctorate such as a DBA, as well as on the characteristics of the doctoral programme itself. These differences are clear in the commonly understood purpose of these two categories of doctoral programme as well as in the motivations of those individuals undertaking them.

As discussed in the introduction, PhD programmes have historically been understood as a means of making a transition into an academic career (Kot & Hendel, 2012). Indeed, research consistently shows that people are often driven to take a PhD by their desire to work as a researcher in academia, as well as interest in the research topic and a desire for personal academic accomplishment (Boman et al., 2021). Therefore, the PhD programme is often seen as the means to facilitate a career change from an industry-based or practice-focused career to one as an academic or as a route into an academic career post undergraduate study. In support of this, Diamond et al. (2014) found that mid-career PhD entrants (those who took a PhD mid-way through their career) did so specifically to change careers into academia.

The decision to take a professional doctorate such as a DBA is also often driven by individual-level motivations such as the desire to develop skills and capabilities or to progress in one's career. An analysis of the motivations given by applicants to our own DBA programme included a range of skills and attributes that individuals wanted to develop, including the ability to bring rigour to their practice, develop thinking skills, access managerial knowledge, and learn research or knowledge sharing skills (Parry & Ryals, 2014). While this is only one programme, our interviews for this book and informal discussions with directors of other DBA programmes suggest that these are typical. On the one hand, these motivations are similar to those of PhD researchers. On the other, the context in which DBA researchers wish to apply their skills and the nature of the career progression that they seek can be very different. Most individuals who study a DBA have little intention of a move into academia full-time (although they may later decide to do so), and instead wish to improve their skills and prospects within their existing occupation. Aligned with this, applicants to the UK-based DBA mentioned above showed motivations related to career progress such as taking on larger roles in their companies. This was often linked to a desire for greater recognition in their company or field or making a broader contribution to their organisation, industry or practice generally.

These motivations are a reflection of the broader purpose of the two types of doctoral programme (PhDs and DBAs). The differences between these programmes, the skills that are developed and the types of employment that they prepare graduates for can be better understood through a consideration of the nature and objectives of the two programmes.

Impact on individual skills and personal qualities

One purpose of any doctoral programme is to develop the technical skills needed to undertake academic research. Feedback from PhD students confirms this, with research demonstrating their confidence in being prepared for an academic career and their efficacy in relation to analytical, technical and data skills and in presenting or writing for academic audiences (Cornell, 2020). Similarly graduates of professional doctorates have been shown to have gained technical research skills. For example, Creaton and Anderson (2021) provided detailed qualitative research on the skills developed by 25 graduates of one professional doctorate in the UK. They noted that these graduates developed research-based and dissemination skills, including undertaking qualitative and quantitative research, critical thinking and finding, assimilating and evaluating evidence. So, on the one hand, the impact of doctoral study on individual skills development is espoused to be similar. Regardless of whether an individual undertakes a PhD or DBA, he/she is expected to leave the programme with a set of skills related to academic research and dissemination. On the other hand, whether these skills are developed across all students or all programmes is dependent on a multitude of factors – not least individual motivation and ability, the design of doctoral programme and the quality of supervisory and other support. Indeed, one of our interviewees expressed concern about the proliferation of poor-quality doctoral programmes and the impact of this on the quality of doctoral graduates entering both the academic and broader labour market.

There is a more significant question in relation to whether these skills will be useful once an individual has completed his/her doctorate and thus whether the doctorate will really have a positive impact on an individual's employability and career prospects. For a doctorate to have a positive impact on employability, the individual must develop skills that are transferable to their future work context and be able to apply these effectively in that environment. This raises a question of 'what are we training doctoral graduates for?'. Any effective programme should take steps to develop skills that will be valuable in an individual's future career whether this is academic or otherwise.

PhDs are typically designed as a means of developing future academics and are often seen as an 'apprenticeship' to becoming an independent academic researcher. For example, Yazdani and Shokooh (2018: 42) describe how the completion of a PhD *"results in the formation of an independent scholar with a certain identity and level of competence"*. For those PhD graduates who do go on to have academic careers, the skills that they have developed through a PhD are likely to be invaluable, laying the foundation for them to be successful in academic research and publications at least, and potentially having scholarly impact. It is worth commenting here that not all PhD programmes support students in developing other academic skills such as those in teaching and learning support, or other administrative and management roles in universities. While PhD candidates in the USA and in some parts of Europe are expected to teach as part of their programmes, this is less often the case in countries such as the UK, meaning that graduates might struggle to transition into academic careers that are focused on teaching and education. Anecdotally, doctoral graduates entering academia may feel ill-equipped to teach or to undertake research that extends beyond the necessarily limited focus of their doctoral studies.

The development of academic research skills might only be impactful for those graduates who enter academic careers. Several authors have noted the lack of academic or research jobs available for PhD graduates and the increasing numbers of PhD students who are gaining employment out of universities. For example, an analysis of data from the Destinations of Leavers from Higher Education (DLHE) Longitudinal survey showed that less than a third of those graduating from Social Science PhD programmes, and of those employed outside of academia, were employed within academia, and less than a third were in a research-related roles (Hanson, 2020). This has led to debates about the value of the skills that doctoral students bring to the economy outside their academic roles (Diamond et al., 2014; Leitch, 2006) and to questions regarding the focus of the PhD on academic research and skills. There is a growing recognition that for PhD programmes to have a positive impact on their graduates' employability, they need to also meet the needs of an employment market outside academia (Halse & Mowbray, 2011).

PhD programmes have been criticised for their failure to provide the transferable skills needed for employability outside academia (Kehm, 2004; Nerad, 2004). In the UK, this has led to a push over the past 15 years to develop transferable skills within PhD programmes to meet the needs of employment markets. In the UK, a report by the then Secretary of State recommended that transferable skills training be included in postgraduate research programmes as standard (Smith, 2010). Despite these efforts, this challenge remains. Recent research in Europe (Boman et al., 2021) found that, while most doctorates offer transferable skills training, these focused on academic rather than broader skills. This survey also found, however, that the skills that doctorate holders had on graduation did match those needed for employment although some skills mismatches did exist, particularly related to doctorate holders having a higher level of academic or research skills than they needed for their job.

The limited impact of PhD qualifications on the employability of graduates outside of academia might be related to the difficulties that many individuals experience in transitioning from PhD students to non-academic jobs and the challenge of applying the skills that they have developed during their doctorate outside academia (Skakni et al., 2022). Along these lines, the Economic and Social Research Council (ESRC) (2021a: 7) recently noted that "*current training does not systematically equip students with skills and attributes such as project and budget management, business/commercial acumen and the ability to communicate with a broad range of audiences*" and recommended that all PhD students developed core skills to help them apply their research skills across both academic and non-academic settings.

The concern about the failure of PhD programmes to develop transferable skills for non-academic careers has contributed to the development of professional doctorates (Kot & Hendel, 2012) that are designed specifically for those planning to enter, or stay in, non-academic careers and therefore aim to provide a wider range of professional skills. Many Higher Education institutions have recognised the opportunity to benefit financially from this need through the provision of DBA programmes at a higher price than PhD programmes. There is a clear point of difference therefore between the objectives of these programmes in relation to their impact on employability and skills. Professional doctorates, including the DBA, focus clearly on developing employability and career development outside of academic careers. Indeed, the outcomes of professional doctorates are generally aimed towards practical application and the workplace (Dos Santos & Fai Lo, 2018; Fenge, 2008; Usher, 2002). Another important distinction is that those entering a DBA usually have considerable practical experience and may already have a high level of work-related skills. Therefore, the design of DBA programmes focuses often on equipping students with skills in developing and using evidence that can help them to make better quality decisions in their work context. In this sense, the impact of a professional doctorate on individual competence is often distinguished as being about developing a 'researching professional' (i.e., someone who uses research skills within his/her professional role) rather than the 'professional researcher' that emerges from a PhD (Bourner et al., 2001: 5). A question that arises here is whether DBA or other professional doctorate programmes really achieve these aims, or whether they actually fail to differentiate themselves from a PhD programme in relation to content or perspective. Our own experience would suggest that DBA programmes often focus on the skills needed for scholarly impact and therefore the '*person*' outcomes of these programmes end up as more like a PhD programme than the alternate objectives above might suggest.

Both PhD programmes and professional doctorates are proposed to also have an impact on the personal qualities of individuals, outside research skills. For example, PhD graduates have been reported as developing personal attributes such as resilience, creativity, determination and problem-solving abilities (Halse & Mowbray, 2011; Kearns et al., 2008; Lovitts, 2005; Mowbray & Halse, 2010). DBA graduates have been found to leave their doctoral programme with increased empathy as the result of examining multiple perspectives on their issue (Hay & Samra-Fredericks, 2019), as well as improved self-actualisation, self-construction and an increased capacity for self-reflection (Burgess et al., 2013; Burgess & Wellington, 2010; Wellington & Sikes, 2006). These potential changes in the mindset and approach of professionals undertaking a DBA have encouraged scholars to investigate the potential personal and identity transitions of DBA researchers. These aspects will be discussed in Chapter 5.

Impact on career progression

Our discussion of the motivations of doctoral candidates earlier in this chapter illustrated that many individuals enter a doctoral programme due to the expected impact on their career, whether that career is in academia or elsewhere. For example, most PhD students believe that their doctorate will positively impact their career prospects (Cornell, 2020). There is some evidence that these expectations might be realised, with research that has found a positive impact of doctoral education on graduate's careers. Diamond et al. (2014) found that a large majority of their survey respondents (87%) believed that their PhD had helped them progress towards their long-term career ambitions. In addition, a large-scale survey by Boman et al. (2021) found that two-thirds of the doctoral graduates surveyed agreed that their programme had made a difference to their career path regardless of the career path chosen. Despite this, questions were raised in the same research about the quality of career support provided in such programmes with only half of the respondents satisfied with the preparation provided for academic careers and only a third satisfied with the preparation provided for non-academic careers. This evidence, alongside the concerns raised by the Leitch (2006) and ESRC (2021a) reviews about the ability of PhD graduates to apply their skills in a non-academic setting, suggests that a large proportion of PhD students at least may leave their programmes dissatisfied and perhaps ill-prepared for future work. A question that we might raise here is whether universities, and doctoral supervisors in particular, are really equipped to provide the support needed for the development of the transferable skills required for non-academic careers, particularly those at a senior level.

Opinions of the impact of doctoral programmes on individuals' careers are clearly mixed. Generally, PhD graduates have a high rate of employment and seem to find jobs relatively quickly after completing their doctorate (Diamond et al., 2014; Hnatkova et al., 2022). For example, a survey by DocEnhance (Boman et al., 2021) found that 72% of PhD graduates in Europe already had a job at the time of completing their PhD, and another 15% had a job within three months. It is also noted that most PhD holders work in careers related to the subject matter of their degrees (Hnatkova et al., 2022). However, as already noted, PhD graduates might not find employment within Higher

Education, with a lack of available job opportunities to meet the available supply. Research has suggested that around half of graduates across all PhDs (Hnatkova et al., 2022) and two-thirds of graduates from Social Science PhDs (Hanson, 2020) work in non-academic sectors. PhD graduates are also notoriously subject to precarious working contracts with a high proportion (20%–49%) of PhD graduates employed on temporary contracts (Boman et al., 2021; Hnatkova et al., 2022), and to working in jobs for which they are overqualified (Boman et al., 2021). In addition, recent evidence has highlighted the pressures resulting from academic careers and the high incidence of burnout and mental health problems (UKCGE, 2021; Urbina-Garcia, 2020). This evidence suggests that the notion of a PhD as a career path to a rewarding academic career may be an illusion for many, although on a positive note, PhDs can provide access to a range of other (non-academic) careers (Hnatkova et al., 2022).

Professional doctorates such as DBAs can also have a positive impact on individuals' careers, although there is generally less evidence available of the career outcomes of a DBA. Entrants to DBA programmes tend to be relatively senior and to have several years of work experience already; therefore, they are often seeking advancement in seniority or a change in role from their doctoral studies. Creaton and Anderson (2021) noted an impact of professional doctorates on participants' self-confidence and self-efficacy, which included having the confidence to apply for other roles and take on additional responsibilities. This is likely to also be true of PhD graduates. It is worth noting that, in our own experience, DBA candidates often already have a high level of self-efficacy and self-confidence on entry to their doctoral programme, so it is difficult to isolate any impact of the programme itself. Creaton and Anderson (2021) also found that graduates of professional doctorates felt that the programme had 'opened doors' career wise and widened their career options. This could, of course, include the decision to change career track to one that focuses on an academic role.

Our own research would suggest that completing a DBA provides a useful platform for senior practitioners to develop their careers. Of the 33 alumni that we interviewed, we saw a variety of career paths post-DBA, including those who moved to more senior positions within the same or different organisations and many who set up their own consultancy businesses based on the knowledge that they had obtained through the DBA. Our interviewees described how the development of research skills, the change in their approach to problem-solving and the increased confidence and credibility that they obtained from their studies had helped to move their careers forward. The impact of the DBA is explained clearly by one of these alumni:

> I think the main impact of the DBA was to provide confidence, undoubtedly it provided confidence. It provided me with some models and frameworks, but I also developed my own model and framework for looking at

things. In meetings or when we were doing some research of our own it gave me a way of categorising things and thinking about things, and relating them to the outside world, and how the outside world might react to that. So, it's made me a much stronger leader as a result, and I am pretty categorical, I wouldn't have done and achieved what I have if I hadn't done the DBA, it's as profound as that.

In sum, it is clear that doctoral education potentially has a positive impact on skills, employability and career progression at an individual level. However, it is important to note that this impact is ultimately dependent on the design of the doctoral programme and the quality of the supervision and support provided. It would be wrong of us to suggest that everyone undertaking a doctorate will see improved career outcomes or employability. Indeed, one of the faculty members that we interviewed as part of our research for this text highlighted the variable quality of the training available as part of doctoral programmes:

> if you look across the sector, I think the training is variable at best and in some places it's absolutely appalling, if there is any at all.

Undertaking a doctoral programme that does not provide an appropriate level of training and development might have a negative impact on an individual's career and employability in the long term. This interviewee went on to explain that in this case there is a negative impact of the doctoral programmes as the graduates are afforded a level of credibility that their research skills do not deserve. They can be allowed to produce poor-quality academic work, to teach and also to supervise future doctoral candidates when they do not have the skills to do so, meaning that the impact of undertaking a substandard doctoral programme (PhD in this case) can have an adverse impact on others outside of that individual.

While many programmes provide excellent research and transferable skills, through the application of tools such as the Vitae Researcher Development Framework (Vitae, 2011), others do not. There was a suggestion from some interviewees that UK and other European programmes are sometimes inferior to North American programmes in relation to the provision of research and analysis training, but the picture is not as simple as this division, with perceived variability in the quality of training within countries. The design of doctoral programmes will be discussed in detail in Section 3, but it is worth noting here the importance of considering skills and employability outcomes outside those needed for completion of the doctorate in the programme design, and of providing adequate career support for those leaving both PhD and DBA programmes. It is only through the careful design of doctoral training and adequate career support that a positive impact of doctoral study on careers and employability might become more uniform.

Points to ponder

1 How does your doctoral programme equip graduates for different career paths?
2 How can supervisors contribute more effectively to the skills development of doctoral students? Should this be part of the supervisor's role?
3 How can non-research skills be evaluated through the doctoral thesis and oral examination? What other ways of assessing these skills are there?

5 Impact on the individual – identity transitions

Introduction

In this chapter, we continue our focus on the person as the outcome of doctoral study. In Chapter 4, we focused on the impact of PhD and DBA study on the skills, employability and career progression of individuals. In this chapter, we move away from these extrinsic outcomes of a doctorate to consider the more fundamental change that a doctoral graduate might experience – to their identity, mindset and sense of self.

Identity can be defined as "*...the ongoing mental activity that an individual undertakes in constructing an understanding of the self that is coherent, distinct and positively valued*" (Alvesson et al., 2008: 15). Scholars have noted that doctoral education is "*as much about identity formation as it is about knowledge production*" (Green, 2005: 153), and yet we seldom discuss the impact of undertaking a doctorate on who a person is or on his/her approach to work and life.

The idea of identity transition is inherent in the notion of a PhD as an apprenticeship for a career in academia, specifically in the idea that an individual moves from being a student to being an academic. Often this is contained in the idea of moving towards independence as a researcher, not only as the result of gaining the research skills needed but also through a change in an individual's understanding of who they are as a person. For example, Lariviere (2012: 464) described the experience of doing a PhD as "*the psychological transition from a state of being instructed on what is already known to a state of personally discovering things that were not previously known*". This is akin to Lave and Wenger's (1991) notion of legitimate peripheral participation in a community of practice, where the novice (in this case the PhD student) moves from the periphery towards the centre of an academic community of practice, as he/she gains knowledge and experience. This trajectory is significant for those doctoral students embarking on an academic career but may be less important for those studying for a DBA who are embedded in other networks of practitioners that are significant for their career choice.

DOI: 10.4324/9781003342014-7

The point here is that a doctoral programme can lead to a transformation not only in relation to what somebody does and how they do it but also in who that person is. Some might argue that this is the most important impact of a doctorate – the impact on the person themselves and how they see themselves. It might certainly be the most profound if an individual's sense of self is significantly altered as the result of doctoral study, particularly as we might expect this change to be enduring and to have impact over several decades.

Generally, doctoral research is seen as being a *"process of transformation and identity development beyond that of an undergraduate or masters level student"* (Coffman et al., 2016: 30). PhD students are assumed to forge their identities to gain membership of the academic community and therefore to construct and reconstruct a range of identities during their doctoral journey (Feng Teng, 2020) to reach this end point.

Similarly, individuals undertaking a professional doctorate such as a DBA are also expected to undergo a transformation in relation to their work-related identities (Philpott, 2015) and to move away from their perspective as a practitioner to develop a more academic approach to evidence-based research (Salipante & Smith, 2012). In this case, DBA researchers can be said to experience a transformation from being an expert practitioner to a practitioner scholar, described as *"actors who have received traditional academic training and who apply their knowledge of theory and research to an organisation's particular challenges to resolve business problems"* (Tenkasi, 2011: 212). In support of this, Simpson and Sommer (2016: 579) suggested that *"the practice of professional doctorates often feels more like a journey leading to some form of metacognitive shift from a problem-solving mindset to a more critical appreciation of different ways of knowing"*.

There appears therefore to be some agreement that this identity transition or transformation occurs in all forms of doctoral education, with the identity label of being a 'researcher' accumulated and assimilated via an individual's experiences during their doctorate (Banerjee & Morley, 2013; Murray & Cunningham, 2011). However, there is less understanding of the nature of this transition or how it occurs. Generally, the literature assumes that doctoral researchers make a linear transition either from a PhD student to an academic or (in the case of DBA researchers) from a managerial identity to the identity of a 'researching professional' (Bareham et al., 2000), or 'reflective practitioner' (Sambrook & Stewart, 2008). However, the idea of a straight line from practitioner or student to academic or scholarly practitioner is simplistic and fails to reflect the difficulties that many doctoral researchers experience in negotiating the transformation. The literature has also failed to consider a more negative effect of doctoral programmes on identity – what if the doctorate shatters an individual's sense of self and that individual does not manage to rebuild it? Our understanding of the possible different impacts of a doctorate on identity is limited.

The doctorate as identity work

It can be argued that doctoral researchers undergo 'identity work' (Brown, 2015) in making the transition to academic (PhD) or scholarly practitioner (DBA). Identity work refers to the way in which people create, adapt, claim and reject identities (Brown, 2017). Generally, management education and business schools have been identified as providing a safe space for identity work to be undertaken (Hay, 2014; Petriglieri & Petriglieri, 2010), with scholars suggesting that management education can have a "*catalytic impact on identity*" (Kempster, 2009: 34) and that participation in a management programme (such as an MBA) can be a step to developing a new work identity (Ibarra, 2003) and lead to an enhanced sense of self (Hay & Hodgkinson, 2008). In line with these arguments, and the growing recognition of doctoral education as a driver of identity transformation, we suggest here that doctoral researchers undergo identity work that results in the transformation of their identity during their doctoral studies. This transformation may be more profound than those experienced on other development programmes because the doctoral process lasts longer and requires an engagement with ontology and epistemology that is unique to doctoral-level study.

An exploration of the wider literature on identity work during management development programmes might provide some insights into the mechanisms behind identity work and transformations during a doctoral programme. Kets de Vries and Korotov (2007) suggested that a development programme needs to go beyond intellectual knowledge transfer and have an emotional impact for identity transformation to occur. They suggested that a development programme should act as an "identity laboratory" (p. 378) that provides individuals with the opportunity to play, climb out of their day-to-day routine and to test new identities before taking them to the real world. This is similar to the concept of liminality (Beech, 2011; Van Gennep, 1960) in which an individual is between two different identities as part of an identity transition or transformation. In the case of Business and Management doctoral programmes, the state in which a doctoral researcher is between student and academic, or between practitioner and practitioner-scholar, could be described as liminal. Scholars have suggested that being in a liminal state is emotionally uncomfortable as the original identity is threatened and the individual will need to undergo identity work to continually transform, to strive for coherence and distinctiveness (Sturdy et al., 2006). Petriglieri and Petriglieri (2010) have suggested that management education can provide both the destabilisation to trigger identity work and the safe environment and sentient community that allows individuals to undergo identity transformations effectively.

Research has suggested that PhD students undergo identity work to construct and reconstruct their identities from student to academic during their doctoral journey (Archer, 2008; Beauchamp et al., 2009; Feng Teng, 2020). As people gain more exposure to the academic community, they experience integration and empowerment as an academic and thus transform from students to scholars (Kasworm, 2010). Less is understood about the identity work that DBA students undertake, although Hay and Samra-Fredericks (2016) have previously conceptualised the DBA journey as liminal. They note that, whereas a PhD student may transform his/her identity to one of an academic, the DBA researcher never completes his/her separation from his/her practitioner identity instead of oscillating between this role and his/her new role as a scholar-practitioner, student and future researching professional, thus staying therefore within a liminal space. The uncertainty and insecurity driven by occupying a liminal space can be stressful and emotional. For example, Hay and Samra-Fredericks (2016) note that DBAs transforming their identity by negotiating "monsters of doubt" experience feelings of confusion, doubt and frustration (Hawkins & Edwards, 2015) as part of this process. Identity transitions driven by management education are emotional and challenging (Kets de Vries & Korotov, 2007; Petriglieri & Petriglieri, 2010; Sturdy et al., 2006).

Our interviews with DBA alumni provide some evidence that DBA researchers at least might undertake identity work in this way. There is certainly evidence of a change in self-perception as the result of a DBA and that this process of transformation can be challenging and emotional. This process is clear in the testimony of one DBA researcher after completing her DBA. Her first comment below explains the emotional nature of the doctoral experience:

> Academically the whole process of … this sentence needs to be broken up and you need to learn to articulate your ideas very clearly, is painful because I assume naturally that you know what I'm talking about, because I assume that you are a rational, clever human being. This is not the case. Consequently, having a scalpel applied to your thinking that takes it apart, lays it bare and then says, is this what you really mean?….There were times, trust me, when it didn't feel I was skipping on glass, more likely just throwing my entire body onto the sharpest bits…. I didn't know how resilient I could be, in the same way I didn't know how good I could be because I didn't know me. So during the process, as much as I might make light of it and all the rest of it, there have been some awful dark moments where I've thought, I have a paper due, I can't do this.

The same researcher goes onto explain how her identity has changed as the result of this process.

> I would now actually class myself as a scholar practitioner and I'm quite happy with that label, I think that's awesome….To me it means somebody who has effectively been trained academically to the extent that they are able to have validity, credibility and robustness in what they do and what they have, and their approach, and their methods. And because I'm a great believer in evidence-based management, I know how to find that evidence,

I know how to look for it, where to look for it, I know a lot of the questions to ask now -I don't know all of them, I know a lot of the questions to ask - and I know whether I'm being fed bullshit or whether I'm being fed Brucey bonus bits of chocolate basically. To a certain extent I think I expected some of that gift, but in its entirety I don't think I was aware of the extent of the gift.

It would be wrong to suggest that a doctorate will have an identical impact on all researchers. Just as people have different motivations for doctoral study, they will have different endpoints in relation to their roles and identities. Some PhD researchers will decide that academia is not for them, while other DBA researchers will internalise a sense of academic-self and take up roles within universities. For example, an interviewee who led a large DBA programme in the USA explained how several of their graduates have joined the institution in academic teaching or research roles. Alumni of the Cranfield Executive DBA programme have also moved into academic roles, into more senior roles within their existing organisation, to consultancy roles or even moved into politics, supporting the idea that the identity transition resulting from a doctorate does not have a common end point. In fact, an identity transformation is unique to the individual.

Conversely, not all doctoral students will go through a transformation in relation to their identity at all. For example, those PhD students who are currently in an academic post might already see themselves as an academic, and thus, the impact of a doctorate may be to reinforce this existing identity rather than to trigger a transition into different sense of self. There might also be some doctoral researchers who will resist the challenge to their identity. For example, one DBA researcher who eventually failed to complete his/her doctorate successfully described the process of receiving feedback as a 'game' and suggested that he/she just 'played along' rather than reflecting on the experience and what it meant for his/her sense of self.

The role of programme design in identity transition

The impact of a doctoral programme on identity is dependent on individual circumstances, but the design of the programme itself will undoubtedly have an impact. Extant literature highlights a number of processes that are seen as important in the development of identity in doctoral students, including conference presentations, writing papers and peer discussions (Åkerlind, 2008; Archer, 2008; Janta et al., 2014; McAlpine & Admundsen, 2009). We go beyond these ideas to paint doctoral programmes as a potentially fertile space for an individual to reflect on, reconsider and transform their identity. Going back to Petriglieri and Petriglieri's (2010) work, we note that identity transitions in management education more broadly are triggered by some sort of identity destabilisation that occurs within a safe environment with the support of sentient others. Our own work with DBA researchers suggests that doctoral researchers (or at least DBA researchers) often need to reconcile existing expertise and self-perceptions with the realisation that the academic standard is difficult to meet. This, alongside (in DBA researchers specifically) the conflict between practitioner and academic ideals can destabilise the individual's identity and lead them to reflect on who they are and who they want to be in the future. We also propose that their cohort of fellow researchers and the context of the business school provides the safe space and sentient community needed to undergo identity work effectively. However, this is only possible in a programme in which researchers are suitably challenged and where suitable support (including peer support) is provided. We will discuss this in more depth in Chapter 7 on programme design.

The importance of others in driving and supporting the impact of a doctoral programme on identity leads us to consider the importance of supervisors or advisers in this process. Indeed, supervisors have been suggested to play an important part in forming and informing students' identities as researchers (Cotterall, 2015). Supervisors have long been recognised as key to an individual's progress in doctoral education (e.g., Barnes & Austin, 2009; Gonzáles-Ocampo & Castelló, 2019; Overall et al., 2011; Simpson & Somner, 2016), but few scholars have considered their role in the formation of students' identities as academics (in the case of a PhD) or as practitioner-scholars (in a DBA). Taking the DBA researcher quoted above as an example, we can see that the feedback provided by her supervisor led to the destabilisation of her identity as an expert and that this, alongside the development of academic skills, triggered a transition to an identity as a scholar-practitioner. It is not clear, however, whether this was a deliberate tactic from the supervisor or whether the supervisor was even aware of this impact.

Views on the importance of supervisors in identity transformation are not, however, consistent. On the one hand, Mantai (2017) in examining the development of academic identity in PhD students noted that supervisors were not highlighted by the students as being important in this process. On the other hand, Posselt (2018) suggested that faculty mentoring or supervision individualises support for socialisation (identity development) and learning in order to help the student to develop strategies for navigating the sociocultural rules of the academy and manage dissonance between academic and personal values in order to develop his/her sense of self and belonging in academia. Some DBA programmes have taken steps to support personal and identity development explicitly in the programme, through the use of individual or peer coaching and the inclusion of reflective assignments such as video diaries. The effective design of doctoral programmes will be considered further in Chapter 7, but we endorse here the suggestion that the design of doctoral programmes needs to consider not only skills development and the completion of doctoral research itself but also how to best facilitate the positive impact of doctoral programmes on an individual's identity.

Points to ponder

1 To what extent are these identity transitions considered either in your own supervisory practice or in the processes of doctoral education in your business school?

2 Can you identify different identity transitions in those doctoral students you know? How were they evidenced?

3 How might the significance/importance of these identity transitions be evaluated/assessed?

Section 3

Process

6 Supervision and support

Introduction

Supervision is regarded as the single most important factor contributing to the completion of a doctoral thesis and the success of a doctoral student (Johansson & Yerrabati, 2017). Supervisors influence the *product* and shape the *person* through the supervisory process, and consequently have a significant influence on the likely impact of doctoral research. Typically, doctoral supervision is conceptualised as a master-apprentice relationship, but this is increasingly uncommon, and other models of supervision predominate to cope with the greater variety of roles supervisors are expected to perform both by an increasingly diverse doctoral student body and by the institutional environment (Bastalich, 2017; Wright et al., 2007). These create challenges which may not always be addressed by supervisory training programmes. In this chapter, we will consider each of these topics beginning with the nature and purpose of supervision before outlining three different types of supervision and reviewing in more detail the various roles of the supervisor. This leads to an examination of some of the challenges faced by supervisors and the training provided to equip them to perform this exciting and influential role.

Nature and type of supervision

Supervision is "the most variable of all variables" (McAlpine & McKinnon, 2013), and in a survey of European universities in 2021, the quality of supervision was recognised as a key issue (Hasgall & Peneoasu, 2022). There are many supervisors who take pride in their role, care deeply for the work and the doctoral student engaged in the research project and provide extensive support, sometimes at personal cost (UKCGE, 2021). But there are some who do not and others for whom it is merely a part of the academic job. This variety inevitably results in widely different outcomes in terms of both the quality of the work and the efficiency with which it is produced (Bastalich, 2017). It also impacts the experience of the student on his/her doctoral journey (Ali et al., 2016). Supervision plays a crucial role in the progress and eventual success

DOI: 10.4324/9781003342014-9

of the doctoral student (Halse & Malfroy, 2010), and any impact arising from doctoral research.

Guerin et al. (2015) note that doctoral supervision can be found in three forms: the traditional master-apprentice model, team supervision and group supervision. The traditional master-apprentice model is founded on a single dyadic relationship between a student and a supervisor with the intention of creating the next generation of scholars, allowing the academic community to propagate and thrive. Evidently, this has parallels with Lave and Wenger's notion of communities of practice (Lave & Wenger, 1991). The novice researcher legitimately adopts a peripheral position on the edge of the community at the outset of their studies but moves inwards as their experience and knowledge increase. Of course, it is unlikely that many will reach the centre of the community by the time they graduate; nonetheless their centripetal journey will have begun. Supervisors can play a significant role in facilitating this trajectory and impacting the subsequent academic career of the doctoral candidate, and therefore the impact of the programme on the individual. Their role is to support the production of a quality thesis and facilitate the entry of the doctoral student through a series of 'rites of passage' into the wider academic community (Amundsen & McAlpine, 2009; Becher & Trowler, 2001). This mode of supervision is most obviously aligned to the attainment of scholarly impact.

An increasingly common form of doctoral supervision is team supervision (Guerin & Green, 2015), where a number of academics, typically two, ideally with complementary skills and experience, guide the student. Although co-supervision is strongly advocated (EUA, 2022), perhaps often mandated, for example, in Australia where national guidelines have been translated into university policies (Robertson, 2017), it is not without problems. McAlpine and McKinnon (2013) indicate that co-supervision can result in:

i   Fragmentation of supervisory responsibilities, so that no one takes responsibility,
ii Conflicting advice that confuses the student,
iii The absence of an overall perspective on the thesis so that it loses coherence, and
iv Conflict between supervisors, leaving the student stranded.

This description contrasts with the ideal view of supervision noted by Wisker and Robinson (2012: 140):

> The relationship between student and supervisor has often been presented as a naturally harmonious one in which, after well-established ground rules have been agreed, the supervisory journey proceeds in a developmental trajectory in which the student becomes less dependent and more independent, until s/he achieves autonomy and competence. During this time limited period regular meetings and discussions enable enculturation

into research in the discipline, while sound behaviours and interactions enable functional and successful progress.

This suggests an unproblematic relationship which from our experience of directing doctoral programmes is sadly not always the case.

The final form is group supervision, where a single supervisor guides a group of students who collectively support each other through the process. This is perhaps more often seen in professional doctorates (Fenge, 2012), where formalised peer learning affords the mutual sharing of experience and good practices amongst professionals allowing the further development of their expertise, an important component of the degree. And something that many academics, who lack the direct practical experience, are unable to provide. The cohort experiences of students on some doctoral programmes may informally serve the same function. In addition, belonging to a cohort of doctoral students may provide a sentient community that supports the transformation of an individual student's identify (see Chapter 5).

Role of the supervisor

The roles played by supervisors have been investigated regularly, providing a rich description of the variety of tasks they perform and the rationales that lie behind them. It is noteworthy, however, that many of these studies focus on the individual supervisor rather than the team, despite the supervisory role being shared routinely between at least two persons, and on tasks that are likely to lead to scholarly impact or skills development rather than impact on policy or practice.

Supervisors engage with the processes of supervision in diverse ways. Drawing on a common set of activities, they prioritise some tasks over others according to their own beliefs about what supervision is and how it should be performed. In a phenomenographic study of 20 supervisors in three universities in Australia, Wright et al. (2007) identified five different conceptions that PhD supervisors have of their roles, namely Quality Assurer, Supportive Guide, Researcher Trainer, Mentor and Knowledge Enthusiast. The goals and approaches to PhD supervision of these five conceptions are indicated in Table 6.1, and each may contribute more or less to the achievement of impact. For example, the 'Quality Assurer' may focus on doable projects which are unlikely to have impact, while the 'Knowledge Enthusiast' may encourage students to make new discoveries or generate new understandings with scholarly impact. The 'Researcher Trainer' and 'Mentor' to differing extents may develop the individual academic, whereas the 'Supportive Guide' may be open to other forms of personal and professional development. There may, of course, be other conceptions of doctoral supervision that, for example, relate to professional doctorates, but they were not considered in that study.

Table 6.1 Five conceptions of doctoral supervision

Role	Goal	Orientation
Quality Assurer	PhD free of fundamental flaws and timely completion	Functionalist and task orientation through a structured set of activities.
Supportive Guide	PhD achieved through a support network	Functionalist and task orientation but through social support to sustain commitment and enthusiasm.
Researcher Trainer	PhD as the beginning of research career	Aim to equip students with skills and abilities to become competent self-managed researchers. The thesis is not the end point.
Mentor	PhD as moulding quality academic researchers	Partners on a journey in a specific research area.
Knowledge Enthusiast	PhD as a quest to new knowledge and discoveries	Passion for new knowledge through challenging learners' assumptions.

Source: Based on Wright et al. (2007).

Others have also identified different conceptions. Murphy et al. (2007) focus on the supervisors' belief about the role. Is the purpose of the supervisor to direct or to guide? Or should the focus be on the task or the person? These two dimensions of *process* and *product*, respectively, may be combined to create a 2×2 matrix (Boehe, 2016), which suggests the need for a different but appropriate supervisory style for each quadrant reflecting the particular conception of the role (Figure 6.1). Each has a different orientation to impact. Directing (or controlling) approaches take a more instrumental view seeking to deliver an examinable thesis within the time frame (task) or the professional development of the person. Guiding approaches that focus on the task pursue answers to problems that may have a practical impact. Alternatively, guiding approaches that focus on the person deliver impact through the development of the person but may also generate new knowledge achieving scholarly impact. Gatfield (2005) observed that not only may different students prefer different supervisory styles, but also they may prefer different styles at different points in their doctoral journey, in effect, moving dynamically around the matrix. This inevitably requires agile supervisors who are able to adapt their styles to meet the need of the student (and required impact) appropriately at any point in their journey.

Supervisors require other skills too. Different authors emphasise different ones. Pyhältö et al. (2015), for example, categorise the skills according to four primary tasks. These are supervising, coaching, managing the project and also the basic prerequisites of being committed and available. McAlpine and McKinnon (2013) report that resolving bureaucratic problems is a key role of the supervisor. Others, surfacing the perspectives of the student, note the importance of open communication and timely and constructive feedback, strong supportive relationships, expertise in, and passion for, the topic, and mentoring to secure the development of the student (Taylor et al., 2018), while

	Directional • Train / guide • Learning how • Apply knowledge to task	**Contractual** • Guide / shape • Become a researcher • Achieve expertise
Guide		
Control	**Laissez-faire** • Direct / shape • Being taught • Apply information to task	**Pastoral** • Nurture / mould • Being taught • Learn skills

Structure *(Process)* is at left spanning Guide/Control.

Task   **Person**

Support *(Product)*

Figure 6.1 Supervisory style grid (based on Gatfield, 2005, and Murphy et al., 2007).

Nulty et al. (2009) emphasise enthusiasm, passion, respect and appreciation of difference and unselfishness as part of a supervisor's mentoring role.

By contrast, Halse and Malfroy (2010) theorise doctoral supervision as professional work comprising five interrelated facets each with different constituents (Table 6.2). The 'learning alliance' emphasises the implicit contractual arrangement between the supervisor and the student to deliver a high-quality thesis, based on mutual respect, clear communication and a goal orientation. Supervisors who reflect on their practice and apply what they have learnt to other students develop 'habits of mind' allowing them to provide balanced assessments of students' work and constructive feedback. This facet might support the delivery of high-quality products and the successful development of highly performing individuals. Scholarly expertise facilitates the enculturation of the student into the academic community (Lee, 2008), which is especially important for those anticipating an academic career and who may have scholarly impact subsequently. Technê (or craft knowledge) embraces the creative and productive use of expert knowledge and may support the delivery of scholarly and practical impact by the student. Finally, contextual expertise understands how to navigate the current complex institutional and disciplinary requirements for successfully completing a doctorate, while retaining "a sense of the value and purpose of the doctorate and doctoral education as an important area of work" (Halse & Malfroy, 2010: 87) that elevates it above a perfunctory responsibility.

54   *Process*

Table 6.2 Five facets of good doctoral supervision

Facet	*Constituent element*
The learning alliance	• A goal to produce a high-quality thesis • Mutual respect • Flexibility in accommodating circumstances • Commitment to collaborate to achieve goal • Clear communication • Explicit strategies for progressing towards goal
Habits of mind	• Capacity to learn and reflect and make judgements • Interested in student and their work • Responsive to student needs • Balanced judgements about quality • Critical and constructive feedback • Learn from experience and apply to others
Scholarly expertise	• Continuous and fruitful production of knowledge through research • Publish academic articles • Scholarly critique of others' work • Identify research opportunities • Advance one's own thinking
Technê (craft knowledge)	• More than technical skills • Provide or direct to appropriate and necessary skills training • Capacity to write and communicate in ways appropriate to discipline or field • Ability to use resources – databases, IT, equipment • Skills in information management and data analysis • Guide in organising and managing time
Contextual expertise	• Knowledge of institutional and disciplinary context • Understand territory and what is required • Other – reviewing for journals, organising conferences and networking beyond university

Source: Based on Halse and Malfroy (2010).

Challenges of supervision

Supervision is a demanding activity requiring flexibility and adaptability to perform different roles effectively for different students within the constraints imposed by national policies for Higher Education and the local response to them (McAlpine & Norton, 2006).

While acknowledging that the 'one-size-fits-all' approach to doctoral supervision is flawed, the increasing diversity of doctoral degrees and those participating in them inevitably will stretch the adaptability of even the most flexible supervisors. Variation in types of degree, its mode of delivery and the demographics of the student population are the three obvious sources of diversity. Those studying full-time for a PhD and anticipating a career in academia will have very different expectations of their supervisor(s) compared to those studying part-time for a professional doctorate and seeking to enhance their professional skills and advance their career, and perhaps make a difference to practice. Nasiri and Mafakheri (2015) challenge the notion that studying FT and PT are similar and detail the different challenges that may be encountered by PT but not FT students arising from the spatial and temporal separation of student and their supervisor. Deuchar (2008) makes a similar observation differentiating UK students from those from other countries, who may for example expect more frequent meetings and want detailed guidance. As the diversity of the doctoral student body increases so the supervision challenge deepens.

More recently, greater awareness of the pressures experienced by doctoral researchers (Nature, 2019) and the consequent mental health issues has placed more emphasis on the extent and quality of pastoral care provided by supervisors to their students. This is in addition to the main role of the supervisor, which, according to the ESRC (2021b), is to support students in meeting the disciplinary and methodological requirements of the doctorate.

Similarly, concern for the future employability of students post completion adds a further dimension, that of careers advisor, to the role of supervisor. Noticing, of course, that a supervisor's experience of a variety of careers is likely to be limited and not especially useful to those who seek, or ultimately find, employment outside the Higher Education sector. As noted in Chapter 4, more doctoral students find employment outside than inside universities.

Furthermore, rapid advances in digital technologies for the collection, manipulation and analysis of data will make some of the traditional research skills increasingly redundant. The importance of expertise in these approaches will diminish, and new skills will be required. At the time of writing, for example, the development of generative artificial intelligence (such as Chat-GPT) is influencing the nature of research approaches, particularly in relation to identifying and synthesising research evidence. The natural advantage of the supervisor in these skills built from prior experience will be removed, and their ability to guide and support commensurately reduced. Both students and the supervisor will need to learn together to discover what is possible, what is useful and how the information can be interpreted. This profoundly alters the power dynamics in the relationship, which currently favour the supervisor (Hemer, 2012; Riva et al., 2022), creating challenges for both parties.

The growing number of challenges influences the ability of supervisors to meet the desired requirements of the doctorate in terms of both delivering a product that has scholarly and/or practical impact and shaping the individual and providing them with the support they require to develop skills to flourish in their chosen career path. Consequently, the experience of overwork and stress amongst doctoral supervisors in the UK reported recently by UK Council for Graduate Education (UKCGE) (2021) and acknowledged by Economic and Social Research Council (ESRC) (2021b) is perhaps unsurprising. It is, nevertheless, a cause for concern, which finds support from a surprising source. In a report, the UK Government House of Commons Science and

Technology Committee (2013) expressed a concern that an overly aggressive push for impact would risk damaging academic research and the welfare of the research communities (Watermeyer, 2016). For this reason, UKCGE (2021) concluded that an optimal number of doctoral students is four, but we are aware that many academics are encouraged, or perhaps obliged, to carry a larger burden. In part this is because the role of a doctoral supervisor is unrecognised and unrewarded. Supervision of research students in practice falls between the education stream and the research stream of university systems (McAlpine & Norton, 2006) and is consequently overlooked.

Supervisory training

Supervisors typically base their approach to supervision on their own experience, replicating what they experienced as good and rejecting what they found to be unhelpful (Amundsen & McAlpine, 2009). This may be augmented over time with individual experiences of supervision and perhaps examining doctoral students. Such an experiential approach to supervisor training is further informed and oriented by the occasional training session often lasting for only a few hours provided by their university. It is reasonable to question whether this is sufficient for them to provide high-quality support to those they are supervising and satisfy expectations for delivering different types of impact. Perhaps it is, but it is more likely that it is not. However, this raises the thorny issue of what supervisor training should entail. A situation made more complex by the variety of doctoral degrees on offer and the increasing diversity of the student body.

The roles identified by Halse and Malfroy (2010) perhaps provide some guidance on the skills that are required, and these might reasonably form the basis of supervisor training. Alternatively, ESRC (2021a) recommend training in the following:

- Equality, diversity and inclusion issues
- Having difficult conversations
- General Data Protection Regulation (GDPR)
- Coaching skills
- Providing constructive feedback
- Key postgraduate research destinations and the broad range of career possibilities that social science PhDs open up
- Understanding power dynamics
- Mental health first aid.

Furthermore, they expect that these topics should be mandatory for all supervisors as part of a continuing professional development programme. As Lee (2008) noted, much of the proposed training concentrates on functional aspects of the task and relationship and has a compliance focus to ensure that the stipulated processes are being adhered to. While this allows the university to confidently predict the timely completion of an examinable thesis, it says nothing about the possibility of scholarly or practitioner impact. Much less emphasis is placed on how to develop the enculturation and emancipatory aspects of the relationship through appropriate mentoring and support. If impact both scholarly and practical is ultimately achieved through relationships, in either shaping the work or subsequently promoting it, then enculturation is vital.

Wright et al. (2007) advocate an alternative to this task focused, compliance-driven characterisation of the training requirements for doctoral supervisors. Based on their work, they suggest that the starting point for supervisor training should be to surface two things: firstly, what supervisors think supervision is, and secondly, how they believe this should be approached. Each of the five conceptions noted above provides a different response to these questions, which makes the provision of single homogeneous training programme unsatisfactory, if the ambition is excellence in supervisory practice that delivers scholarly, practical and personal impact.

Points to ponder

1 How do the three forms of supervisions influence the achievement of different types of impact? Which aspects do you find most challenging/least challenging?
2 How would the conceptualisations of supervision of professional doctorates differ from those for PhDs?
3 How might supervisory training be developed to encourage the delivery of impact?

7 Programme structure and content

Nature of the doctorate

The PhD is considered to be the premier higher degree (Park, 2005) or the "pinnacle of academic accomplishment" (Nyquist & Woodford, 2000). In its traditional PhD format, the doctorate was historically a qualification to teach others (Jones, 2018), which has changed over time to emphasise research. As a qualification it has a relatively well-understood scope or purpose, even if this is imprecisely defined. However, as we discussed in Chapter 1, around the millennium powerful social and economic forces altered the Higher Education context, and these changes have permitted the proliferation of a range of other doctorates, including professional doctorates like the Doctor of Business Administration (DBA) (Park, 2005). Inevitably this has changed both the scope of the doctorate and the nature of the programme of study.

The increased scope has loosened the certainty over the purpose of the PhD. In their review of US doctoral education, Nyquist and Woodford (2000: 8) define the "PhD as a selective, specialised degree with the singular focus of producing a creative, self-initiating independent scholar and researcher for academia", but then contrast this traditional view with the more contemporary view that it "should produce graduates who can consider an array of options in terms of careers and contribute to society in many ways outside the academy". Similar tensions occur at a policy level within the UK. The valorisation of research (and the written output of the PhD) driven by the periodic national Research Excellence Framework (REF) assessment of university research quality is in tension with the skills development agenda championed by Vitae, and in the Social Sciences by Economic and Social Research Council (ESRC). From an institutional perspective in the UK, the policy guidance demands that high-quality research is delivered as quickly as possible to satisfy the requirements of REF. This risks the development of a 'directorial' style of supervision aimed at managing the project rather than the person (Deuchar, 2008). Moreover, it encourages the selection of risk-free research projects that are less likely to have scholarly impact in the way we have

DOI: 10.4324/9781003342014-10

defined in Chapter 2. In contrast, and simultaneously, there is a requirement to perform well in the annual Postgraduate Research Evaluation Survey (PRES), which requires universities to attend to the wider research culture and environment. Concurrently, the League of European Research Universities (LERU) anticipate a focus on skills development, including intellectual skills, academic or technical skills and personal or professional management skills (LERU, 2010) in order "to tackle major societal challenges" (ESRC, 2021a).

This *product* versus *person* debate has protagonists on either side. For some, 'doctorateness' is found in the *product* – the thesis (Park, 2005) – and not in the *person*. More recently, the European University Association (EUA) considers that "the responsibility of doctoral education is to equip the next generation of academics and other knowledge workers for the challenging roles they will need to play in their future careers" (EUA, 2022: 4). This emphasises the development of the *person*.

According to Åkerlind and McAlpine (2017), doctoral supervisors identify three overarching purposes of a doctorate. These are to enable doctoral students to:

i   Become self-sufficient as a researcher,
ii Become innovative as a researcher, and
iii Develop as an individual.

These have implications for the pedagogical approach to doctoral education. The first encourages training in appropriate skills at the right time (skills development). The second requires providing challenge and opportunities to question (ideas development), in addition to methodological training, while the third encourages more informal interactions to stimulate interest and enjoyment (personal development). Based on the similarity of these outcomes to those in other studies, they suggest the trilogy of purposes of doctoral education might be to serve instrumental, intellectual and altruistic purposes. These all have a *person* rather than a *product* focus. Moreover, these align with definitions of purpose of doctoral education provided by other influential stakeholders. For example, according to LERU (2010: 2), "research and the people trained in it inspire many of the ideas, aspirations and actions that contribute to the vitality of society and its capacity for bold creativity in responding to whatever the future might bring". This is echoed by the EUA (2022) above. The aim of research training is to produce "creative, critical, autonomous, intellectual risk takers" (LERU, 2010: 3). This aspiration to produce highly trained individuals necessarily involves an interplay between professional research experience and personal development. The balance between these activities, however, will vary across the different forms of the doctorate and shape the pedagogical design and the administrative organisation of the programme. We will consider the more significant aspects now.

Recruitment and admission/selection

Finance and funding considerations perhaps dominate every other variable in the decisions surrounding the application to study for a doctorate, influencing where, when, what and how to study. In some European countries, doctoral researchers are often employed by the university contributing more fully to the life of the department than those typically receiving a studentship or bursary to study full-time (FT) and classed as students, as is more common in the UK. This difference can create differences in status, which are reflected in different expectations of the contribution of the candidate to the university. In either case, it is important that sufficient funds are available to ensure a successful outcome (EUA, 2022). Where the outcome is based on publications, funding makes success more likely. Larivière (2013) noted that funded students were more likely to publish than unfunded ones. Without funding students are often obliged to study part-time (PT), needing to find or remain in employment to support themselves. Their prospects of making a scholarly impact are diminished. However, funding for FT students studying in the UK is often limited to three years, which inevitably restricts the scale and scope of any impact.

Concern over the lack of diversity of doctoral researchers and those holding doctoral qualifications provides encouragement for funding to be made available to a wider pool of potential applicants (UKCGE, 2021), enabling the "best intellects to have the opportunity to study" (LERU, 2010), assuming that they are the ones most likely to generate the greatest impact. Nevertheless, recruitment should pay attention to prior knowledge, qualifications, motivations, skills, receptivity to feedback and the propensity for critical thinking. Our experience suggests that interviewing candidates after they have prepared and submitted a written research proposal helps to ensure that prospective doctoral candidates are not set up to fail upon entry to their chosen doctoral programme. Many are deterred by the requirement for a written proposal, which is ironic given the qualification is based on the assessment of a written document.

Assessment

Standards for qualifying for a doctorate frequently embrace the notion of an original contribution to knowledge. For example, the QAA (2018: 1) states that "doctoral degrees are qualifications rooted in original research – the creation of new knowledge or originality in the application of knowledge". The descriptor for a higher education qualification at level eight states that

> Doctoral degrees are awarded to students who have demonstrated:
>
> • The creation and interpretation of new knowledge, through original research or other advanced scholarship, of a quality to satisfy peer review, extend the forefront of the discipline, and merit publication.

- A systematic acquisition and understanding of a substantial body of knowledge which is at the forefront of an academic discipline or area of professional practice.
- The general ability to conceptualise, design and implement a project for the generation of new knowledge, applications or understanding at the forefront of the discipline, and to adjust the project design in the light of unforeseen problems.
- A detailed understanding of applicable techniques for research and advanced academic enquiry.

(QAA, 2014: 30)

However, these descriptions are imprecise and their interpretation in an individual case is variable. Inevitably this raises questions about the consistency of standards between individual outcomes, comparability between institutions (Taylor, 2022) and between nations, and the equivalence between different types of doctorate. In the latter case, although parity is asserted, it is recognised that "the notion of the doctorate varies across, space, time and different disciplines" (Wellington, 2013: 1490). Practices that assure the transparency of the process help mitigate some of this variability. In the UK, these include, for example, independent preliminary reports from each examiner providing an assessment of the work and the presence of an independent chair at the oral examination (Taylor, 2022).

It is, however, worth noting that the assessment of the doctorate is based on the written document and not on the other skills that may have been developed alongside this. Yet these are the attributes valued more strongly in many of the policy documents relating to doctoral education. There appears to be considerable inertia to breaking with the traditional mode of examining doctorates. How we effectively assess the variety of attributes that constitute a successful doctoral graduate remains an unanswered question. Furthermore, the assessment of the doctoral thesis is made by academics. Inevitably this evaluation will privilege the academic aspects of the submitted document and the realised or potential scholarly impact at the expense of practitioner or policy impact. The appointment of senior practitioners or policymakers to evaluate the potential for any practical or policy impact of the research may help to redress this balance, while recognising that the doctorate is an academic qualification.

Institutional provisions

In a recent study, we found that peer networks were valued highly by doctoral students to support them through their PhD journey and that a number of structural items, including shared physical space, enabled these (Pilbeam et al., 2012). To combat isolation, which is strongly present in PT students, a cohort experience, especially in the initial stages configured around research methods training, for example, helped. This unfortunately unravels as time passes, and students' research interests and their pace of progress diverge. Although not always relished, the normative expectation that all students would present their work to each other on more than one occasion during their studies proved invaluable. It helped to clarify the message of the research, enhancing the prospect of scholarly impact, and invariably piqued interest and created contacts between students who had not previously connected, enabling personal development. Structural changes like these provide the 'safe space' within a sentient community for the transformational identity work discussed in Chapter 5 to take place.

Formal progress review processes are common characteristics of doctoral programmes. While they can be a mere administrative formality, and perceived as a nuisance by some, they may also provide the opportunity for a focussed conversation with other academics, including their supervisors, on the topic of interest. Such an experience is also helpful preparation for the final oral examination. These shared experiences lend support to the doctoral students as their studies progress, helping to develop both the product and the person.

Creating an enabling environment, through small changes to an otherwise possibly sterile administrative process, can have a powerful effect, improving the quality and publication potential of the work and so making scholarly impact more likely. Changing the design of the programme can also enable practitioner impact and the development of the person. Boxes 7.1 and 7.2 describe the content of DBA programmes offered by two different UK business schools to, respectively, enable personal development or practitioner impact.

Box 7.1   Design for personal impact

One interviewee explained how the DBA programme at their business school had focused explicitly on the impact on the *person* and particularly on aspects of identity development through the creation of a personal development module. This consisted of a series of exercises and activities designed to encourage people to reflect on themselves and build their self-awareness. For example, in one activity, students were asked to undertake a process called 'Life Histories' in which they wrote chapters about different parts of their lives that had really shaped them. This would be followed by a workshop with an expert facilitator where these life chapters would be discussed. The interviewee described these workshops as very emotional. The psychological safety within the cohort was important to the success of these. The cohort also undertook a series of reflective assignments and received feedback on these from a trained personal development expert to help them build their self-awareness.

Box 7.2   Design for practical impact

The Cranfield DBA was redesigned in 2013 to distinguish it clearly from the PhD programme and to improve the potential for DBA research to have impact on practice or policy. Cranfield School of Management has a strong focus on applied research and practical impact more broadly, so this was in keeping with the institution's existing approach and culture. The design was loosely based upon evidence-based management, encouraging students to identify, collect and evaluate the best available evidence relevant to their research question. In line with the four sources of evidence identified by Briner et al. (2009), students are asked to evaluate existing evidence, collect evidence from stakeholders, consider contextual aspects and draw on their own expertise. Specifically, this re-design consisted of the following elements:

- DBA students are required to develop an "impact plan" alongside their empirical research design. This identifies the practitioners and policy makers who are potential end users of the research and detail a strategy for engagement with these throughout the doctoral studies, and for the dissemination and exploitation of research findings to these groups.
- The final DBA thesis consists of three elements: a literature review; empirical project; and an impact statement. The impact statement details the actual or expected impact of the research, the engagement, dissemination and exploitation to date, and a future strategy for developing impact from the work.
- A module on "Engagement, Influence and Impact" was developed to support the above two activities. This includes aspects such as the development of toolkits of frameworks from research; creating executive development programmes; use of different dissemination channels (e.g., social media, blogs, writing for practitioner media).
- Workshops relating to a number of applied research methods (e.g., case studies, intervention studies) were added to the curriculum.

Skills requirement and training

Specifying the content and designing a training programme that is fit for purpose is challenging: a survey of European universities in 2021 showed that skills training varies reflecting the different disciplinary and university contexts (Hasgall & Peneoasu, 2022). Not only has the scope of such a training programme increased over time, but the diversity of students has increased, and therefore the requirements of such a programme have expanded. Following the Roberts' review (2002), which focused on Science, Technology, Engineering and Mathematics (STEM) skills, training from doctoral programmes in the UK seeking accreditation from ESRC, and thus the eligibility for funded studentships, included not only research methods but transferable skills that included training in interpersonal and communication skills, management and commercial awareness. These were perceived to be neglected. The most recent ESRC review (ESRC, 2021a) now additionally includes digital methods, data management, project and budget management and communication. We might expect skills relating to the use of artificial intelligence to also gain prominence in future guidelines.

In the UK, the ESRC (2021a) encourages institutions to conduct a training needs analysis (TNA), subsequently revised to a development needs analysis (DNA) (ESRC, 2022), for each student at the commencement of their studies, and to continually update this through self-reflection during the course of the degree. This affords the creation of a programme of training and development that is bespoke for each student. Inevitably, that comes at a cost, and the institutional response is often a generic provision provided at regular intervals. Moreover, additional skills training will be required by supervisors to deliver the necessary support for this process. Balancing these conflicting requirements to achieve an optimal outcome, especially one that delivers durable personal impact, is difficult.

A TNA/DNA makes an important assumption that the skills that need development are both recognised and desired, and moreover that they fall within the university's capacity to develop. Numerous lists of skills that should be developed can be found. Patterson et al.'s (2019: 17) model of a 'transformative doctoral education' "envisions discipline specific knowledge coupled with a broader interdisciplinary perspective and addresses the transferrable skills necessary to successfully navigate an ever-changing workforce and global landscape". It is achieved through the development of four key skill sets, namely, awareness and critical reflection, imaginative and creative problem-solving, effective discourse and authentic relationships. Vitae, in the Researcher Development Framework, provided a list of 63 skills descriptors across four domains (Vitae, 2011) in response to the Roberts' review. However, Bryan and Guccione (2018) note that these are still research career focused, and that other skills such as developing cultural awareness, self-efficacy and leadership, are value-adding in the context of a changing career landscape for doctoral graduates. Tailoring of the provision is needed to meet the needs of the student within the capacity of the organisation to deliver.

As the emphasis on interdisciplinary research and the importance of collaborative partnerships with industry and other stakeholders grows (ESRC, 2021a), so the boundary between universities and other types of organisations becomes more porous allowing the fluid movement of individuals between different entities. For FT PhD students, particularly those who are younger, these transitions can be enabled by placements or internships during their doctoral studies. Movement in the other direction, especially for those studying for professional doctorates or PT PhD students already in employment, also needs appropriate support as noted in Chapter 4 and considered above.

Next-level requirements and future direction

Designing doctoral programmes to meet the requirements of students with increasingly different needs and expectations and to respond to policy expectations requires careful thought and reflection given the complex and sometimes conflicting interdependencies. Supervision occurs at the level of the individual and these relationships show infinite variety. Nevertheless, they are constrained within an institutional environment. Each university has its own practices (LERU, 2014), although the influence of this is perhaps not widely understood. Such diversity makes it difficult both to specify and to coordinate the design and support of a system to deliver impact that simultaneously has scholarly impact through high-quality publications that challenge the field (Chapter 2), practitioner impact through revisions to current processes and practices (Chapter 3) and transformative impact on the individual (Chapter 5) and their subsequent career trajectory (Chapter 4). A task that is made more challenging by the ambition for doctoral programmes to be international, interdisciplinary and intersectoral (LERU, 2010). Prescribing a single one-size-fits-all approach to achieve this is infeasible, and appropriate local solutions that resolve these different ambitions in different ways need to be documented.

Points to ponder

1 How does your university resolve the tension between delivery of high-quality theses and high-quality skills? Is one prioritised over the other?
2 Should the assessment of doctorates change to consider (i) the development of skills and (ii) practitioner or policy impact? If so, how?
3 How do the structures associated with the doctoral programmes in your university support the delivery of different types of impact?

8   Conclusions

Introduction

In this book, we have examined the impact of Business and Management doctoral programmes. At the outset, we noted the global importance of this field of study in terms of numbers of programmes and students and questioned the lack of understanding of their impact. Given the investment of both individuals and institutions in such programmes, it is surprising that we know so little about how they influence the academic or practical field or the individuals who undertake them. Against this background, we have explored whether Business and Management doctoral programmes have impact. Using a 3P's framework of product, person and process we have considered what (or who) has changed as a result of this impact and how such impact can be facilitated.

These considerations have not been straightforward. Not only have the doctoral programmes in Business and Management evolved into a variety of different forms and structures, but the impact of these programmes also varies and is often unclear. As noted by MacIntosh et al. (2021), while the achievement of impact sounds relatively straightforward, the relationship between (in this case) doctoral studies and impact is reliant on a dynamic interaction of a multitude of factors, the most important being the expectations of both the student and the supervisor. To tackle this complexity, we have inevitably simplified and generalised. Formerly, the nature of the impact achieved from a doctorate is dependent on the type of doctoral programme undertaken. Here we have divided these broadly into traditional PhD programmes and professional doctorates (most commonly Doctor of Business Administration (DBA) programmes). We recognise the variation within PhD and DBA programmes and that programmes for part-time PhD students might combine elements of both, more or less effectively. Nevertheless, throughout the text, we have made broad comparisons between these two types of doctorate. Our rationale for this comparison is the espoused motivations of PhD and DBA programmes as focused primarily on scholarly or practical impact, respectively.

The book is structured around the type or level of impact that a doctoral programme might have. Firstly, we considered impact derived from the

DOI: 10.4324/9781003342014-11

research itself – or the *product* of doctoral studies. This either drives a change in the academic field (scholarly impact) or influences policy or practice (practical impact). Secondly, we examined impact on, or of, the individual (the *person*) who has completed a doctorate. This can be conceptualised as impact on career or employability, and impact on identity. Thirdly, we examined the *process* by which doctoral studies can facilitate impact through their design and the support and supervision of students.

Throughout this book, we have drawn on available published evidence, interviews with experts and alumni of doctoral programmes, and our own experiences of managing doctoral education over the past 20 years. In doing so, we have taken a questioning and sometimes critical stance, hoping to challenge both the reader with our 'points to ponder' and the rhetoric around the impact that can be achieved from doctoral programmes. We realise this may have created more questions than answers, and so in this chapter we aim to rectify this by not only drawing conclusions but also setting out our suggestions for the direction that doctoral education in Business and Management might take to have greater impact in the future. We begin by drawing the discussions in this book together in relation to the questions posed in our introduction, before setting out our reflections for the future of doctoral education in relation to impact.

Product: does Business and Management doctoral research have impact?

As noted above, identifying impact from doctoral research is neither simple nor straightforward. Not only does the potential impact vary in its focus and nature, but its definition and evaluation are often unclear and problematic. We distinguish here between scholarly and practical or policy-related impact.

Scholarly impact

Beginning with the *product*, doctorates (particularly PhDs) are commonly associated with scholarly impact, through the notion of a contribution to academic knowledge. Indeed, this is the normal requirement for being awarded the qualification. The idea of a contribution often focuses on the need for novelty in the research findings compared to existing research. In fact, it could be argued that Business and Management as a discipline is overly focused on novelty to the exclusion of replication studies that might be equally useful in taking a field forward (Miller, 2007). Novelty is different to impact. If impact drives *change,* then a genuine contribution would need to shape the future of the academic field or alter its direction. As noted earlier, the Economic and Social Research Council (ESRC) (2023) describes academic (scholarly) impact as "shifting understanding and advancing scientific method theory and application". We suggest that while doctorates make an academic contribution through originality or novelty, they rarely have real scholarly impact. It is important to note here that most research published in academic journals also fails to have any scholarly impact. So, the output of doctoral studies is not unique but reflects the disciplinary norms. Furthermore, identifying real change in an academic field can only occur sometime after the research is completed. Our ability to evaluate this in relation to doctoral research is limited and would be an impractical criterion for an examination.

Practical and policy-related impact

Over recent years, government policy in the UK and other countries has driven a greater focus on the need for research, including doctoral research, to have an impact on practice or policy. This raises the important question of what or who the doctorate might impact. For the ESRC, this is about impacting society and the economy and creating benefits for individuals, organisations or nations. In Business and Management, this may arise from influencing management policy and practice by shaping management behaviour (instrumental impact), or reframing management debates or concepts (conceptual impact). While the rhetoric around the impact of Business and Management research (including doctoral research) has certainly increased in recent years, we question the extent to which doctoral research drives such changes. Certainly, while we might accept that the core purpose of a PhD programme is not practical or policy-related impact, the espoused aims of professional doctorates are precisely to produce research with the capacity for such impact. Likewise, many individuals enter DBA programmes with the motivation to solve a management problem and therefore to improve the practice of management. Take for example, our DBA alumna who strived to improve performance management in the public sector (see Chapter 3).

Despite good intentions, there are several factors that impede the achievement of this ambition. Firstly, while the intentions of DBA programmes and researchers often reflect broad ambitions to improve management practice or organisational performance, the programmes themselves are rarely designed to facilitate or support such outcomes. The focus on scholarly contribution as the requirement of a doctorate is prioritised, meaning that most DBA programmes are designed to develop academic research skills and to understand theory to ensure successful completion rather than to secure changes in practice. Our own experience and discussions with DBA alumni suggest that DBA programmes are often designed in ways that reflect PhD programmes and not to support alternative objectives. Secondly, those academics who supervise DBA students have often completed a PhD themselves, spend their days striving for academic contribution through publications and are therefore more familiar and comfortable with research that supports scholarly aims. Indeed, the motivation of faculty to supervise doctoral students is often to achieve academic publications, so it is in their interests to focus on the more scholarly aspects of the work. This can lead to a failure of supervisors – and also other faculty involved in DBA programmes – to drive forward the practical relevance and potential impact of DBA research. These two aspects mean that where DBA research does have practical or policy-related impact, this is often due to chance or efforts on the part of the student.

Thirdly, the policy context for Higher Education in the UK has developed definitions of impact that enable measurement, but these are narrow and restrictive and do not reflect the diversity of impact that is possible from doctoral research. The Research Excellence Framework (REF) focus on reach and significance, for example, belittles the impact that DBA research might have on an individual's single organisation, which may be the primary motivation of a DBA researcher. The focus on narrow definitions of impact can also mean that the potential for broader impact on society as opposed to impact that is measurable is often ignored or curtailed. As Kirchherr (2018) challenged, a PhD should be about improving society, and yet rarely do PhDs address societal issues such as those related to the Sustainable Development Goals (SDGs) or Grand Challenges (Brammer et al., 2019; George et al., 2016). However, this may be unrealistic. Social or organisational problems are typically multidisciplinary (Bastow et al., 2014), and therefore not amenable to doctoral research which has to be narrowly focused to evidence a clear scholarly contribution.

It is noteworthy that, as with scholarly impact, an evaluation of practical impact as part of the assessment for a doctoral qualification is generally impractical due to the length of time needed for impact to be realised. Consequently, it is more important to consider whether impact can be generated or developed during a doctorate not whether it can be assessed. In the Cranfield DBA programme, practical relevance and the potential for impact are encouraged through early engagement with potential end users of the findings, dissemination and exploitation of the work through practitioner events and publications, and development of toolkits, frameworks or programmes. The achievement of practical or policy-related impact requires not only a different approach to research and a different set of research skills to be developed, but it also requires time and additional effort. In recent years, we have seen pressure on business schools to provide shorter doctoral programmes, and funding to support doctoral studies is commensurately limited. In the UK, full-time PhDs are now usually three years, and DBAs four years part-time. In the USA, DBAs are usually only three years part-time. These relatively short periods of time preclude taking the steps needed to disseminate and exploit research findings with potential beneficiaries, and consequently curtail impact. Nevertheless, as we have shown in Chapter 3, doctoral research does have practical impact, but this happens not because a doctoral researcher begins with a practical topic or motivation, but because the process – the design of the programme and support offered – enables rigorous and relevant research.

Person: who do doctoral programmes have impact on?

Individual (person)-level impact

General discussions of the impact of Business and Management research have focused on either scholarship or practice. Inevitably, this will also be a consideration for doctoral research. However, a far greater impact of doctoral programmes is on the individual researcher. Indeed, the evidence discussed in this book suggests that doctoral graduates often undergo significant changes in their mindsets and identities which can change their approach to problem-solving, decision-making and work. For those on a PhD, this might enable them to transition into an academic role, while for DBA graduates it might enable them to adopt a more rigorous or evidence-based approach in their practical work, thus allowing them to deal better with the complexity and challenges of senior positions. These transformed individuals may subsequently have a significant and often beneficial impact on their scholarly or practical domains. Therefore, we posit that the most notable impact from doctoral programmes is both on – and via – the individual doctoral graduate. This should not be a surprise. The UK Quality Code for Higher Education (QAA, 2014) clearly states individual-level learning outcomes related to doctoral education (regardless of doctorate type), which include the ability to:

- *Make informed judgements on complex issues in specialist fields, often in the absence of complete data and be able to communicate their ideas and conclusions clearly and effectively to specialist and non-specialist audiences.*
- *Continue to undertake pure and/or applied research and development at an advanced level, contributing substantially to the development of new techniques, ideas and approaches.*

Despite this clear expectation that doctorates develop individuals, doctoral programmes still tend to focus largely on the production of the thesis (the *product*) rather than the development of the *person*. While we acknowledge that most programmes aim to develop broader research skills, the focus is principally on equipping students to undertake their research and deliver a thesis, and not on the transformation of the individual. Even with UK research councils' encouragement to introduce a Development Needs Analysis (DNA) for each doctoral student, the learning outcomes as stated by the Quality Assurance Agency for Higher Education, UK (QAA) are rarely (if ever) assessed outside an evaluation of the product. The implicit assumption is that the impact of the doctoral programme on the person is evidenced through the thesis, and that if an individual can demonstrate and defend a contribution to knowledge at a particular point, they must also have developed the skills and competencies required in a doctoral graduate, and that these will endure. We would suggest that this is not necessarily the case. Moreover, until doctoral programmes focus more clearly on the person rather than the product (like the one described in

Chapter 7), the ability to satisfy the QAA's learning outcomes for doctoral education is unlikely to be realised and the opportunity for achieving significant impact missed.

Individual (career)-level impact

The evidence discussed in this book suggests that the impact of doctoral education on an individual's skills, employability and career is mixed, depending on the nature and quality of training provided. The PhD is generally conceptualised as the route into an academic role, but do PhD programmes genuinely equip graduates with the skills that they need for an academic career? Most PhD programmes provide research skills training, but graduates' experience of applying such skills is often limited to those specific techniques used for their own doctorates, and these may not have been well performed. Furthermore, it is questionable whether the traditional research skills taught in many programmes will be fit for purpose in the future given the growth of generative artificial intelligence and other advances. In addition, doctoral graduates in the UK may leave with only a narrow understanding of their subject, unlike those in the USA, where PhD candidates are expected to undertake modules in their broader subject before moving to the research phase of their doctorate. More significantly, UK PhD programmes rarely provide training in the other non-research-related skills that an individual might need for an academic career. Analogous to a triathlete, an academic requires skills in research, teaching and generating impact, but most PhD programmes only equip graduates with one of these skills – research, paying little or no attention to the other two. This is problematic for those embarking on teaching-focused academic careers which often require a PhD as an entry criterion. The value of the PhD and the impact of a doctoral programme on academic careers and employability may be more limited than expected.

Finally, impact is normally conceptualised as a positive change, but this is not always the case. In recent years, concerns have grown about the wellbeing and mental health of doctoral (particularly PhD) students as pressures to publish and obtain an academic post take their toll. Negative effects at an individual level may be paralleled at a sector level. New academics who lack skills and understanding of practical and policy-related impact are unlikely to develop such capabilities in the doctoral students that they supervise, ensuring that scholarly contributions will continue to be prioritised and other forms of impact neglected. Perpetuating this problem might be avoided if doctoral programmes took a broader view of impact.

The way forward – a short manifesto for impact from doctoral programmes

The foregoing analysis of the impact from doctoral programmes may seem negative: actually, we retain our belief that doctoral education has the potential for significant and positive impact on individuals, policy and practice and society, more broadly. Our purpose in this section is to urge those who lead doctoral education – whether at an institutional or sector level – to take action and to be more deliberate in their design and management of programmes to facilitate impact. In this section, we briefly outline some suggestions for how this might be achieved.

Design for impact

It is time for doctoral programmes to explicitly consider different types of impact and how the potential for these can be facilitated through the appropriate design of programmes and the supervision and support offered to doctoral students. We recommend a differentiated approach. The type of impact focused on should reflect the fundamental nature of the doctoral programme and the motivations of those who undertake them. Now maybe the time to consider what a doctoral level contribution of a professional doctorate could look like and to develop a common understanding of this across the sector so that the current situation where contributions from DBA and PhD programmes are so similar can be avoided.

For PhDs, a focus on scholarly contribution (and future scholarly impact) is appropriate alongside the development of academic skills. These skills and capabilities should be broader than those needed for the specific research to be undertaken and should also include those needed for an academic career such as teaching and learning. It may be important that these are assessed. Often these researchers are full-time, so sufficient funding needs to be available for them to have time to complete their thesis as well as acquire the wider skills to the appropriate level.

For DBAs, or other professional doctorates, a focus on practical or policy-related impact that is broadly defined is crucial. DBA researchers enter a programme with the desire to change something about their domain of practice and to accelerate their practice-focused career. Those designing DBA programmes should consider how students can be supported to engage with the beneficiaries of their research and to disseminate and exploit it effectively. Additionally, for both DBA students and those PhD students who will not enter academic careers, the provision (and assessment) of transferable skills is important.

Focus on the person

A clear message from our discussion above is the need to pay more attention to the *person* as an output of a doctoral programme rather than only the *product*. As suggested above, the best potential for impact from doctoral programmes appears to be for impact either on or via the individual doctoral student, rather than of the research itself. Our research provided numerous examples of doctoral graduates who have gone on to have a significant practical impact on their organisation, sector or field.

In our discussion above, we have alluded to a few directions that this focus on the person might take. More deliberate attempts to develop transferable skills are needed, whether these are academic or broader transferable skills regarded as important by organisations. This is not to diminish the research or the training in research skills, but perhaps to use the research process as a form of experiential learning where the focus is shifted to include the individual rather than focusing solely on the thesis. This development should be accompanied with some evaluation or assessment to ensure that the learning is broader than the capacity to undertake and defend a single research project. Thus, the submission of the thesis could be accompanied by a reflective portfolio, and the *viva voce* might involve the assessment of these learning outcomes as well as the defence of the thesis. PhD or DBA students should be required to demonstrate the ability to be independent scholars or researching professionals as appropriate. Many academics would claim that this should be the focus of existing doctoral programmes, but we believe that it represents a shift and one that would require some rethinking of doctoral-level assessment, perhaps to include responses to hypothetical scenarios. This would necessarily also require the development of faculty as supervisors or examiners.

Care for the supervisor

Doctoral supervision is critical to the success of the doctoral researcher. The growing diversity of the student body and the variety of doctoral programmes in Business and Management places increasing strain on supervisors. One of the key competencies required of doctoral supervisor noted in Chapter 6 is the ability to adopt approaches or styles that are appropriate to the individual. As the expectations multiply and diverge, satisfying them all becomes infeasible. Our earlier suggestions around evaluation criteria would clearly add to this burden. A response might be for supervisors to focus on particular degree formats (PhD or DBA but not both). This would allow them to develop expertise relevant to the degree and reduce the overall workload associated with managing a greater diversity of needs.

In addition, it is important that supervisors receive better training. Rather than relying on their own experience, and any input gleaned from short formal training sessions, which typically last for at most half a day, training should be more extensive. This is especially the case if it is to satisfactorily meet the additional requirements of experiential learning and personal development noted above.

Structural changes within universities may also help to provide greater recognition of the supervisor role, which is often overlooked. Doctoral supervision sits in an ambiguous position between the common university silos of research and teaching (or education). Consequently, it is subject to conflicting policy demands that emphasise high-quality research outputs, the development of skilful individuals and the creation of vibrant research cultures, amongst other things. These competing tensions make effective supervision, which pays attention to the individual student, challenging.

Address societal issues

The clamour for practical or policy impact from research in Business and Management, and in other disciplines too, continues to grow. What is curious is the apparent reticence to engage with those topics that are widely acknowledged to be the most significant and likely to generate the greatest impact. Examples of these include the UN SDG, and other grand challenges including the migrant crises in Asia and Europe, climate change-induced natural disasters, scarcity of water and food or the consequences of nascent technologies such as the 'internet of things', machine learning and artificial intelligence for work, organisations and institutions. Instead, we debate their meaning and the approaches we might adopt (Brammer et al., 2019; Kunisch et al., 2023; Seelos et al., 2023). Research-based evidence that helps to tackle social inequalities has potential to make a major impact. Similarly, leadership and change in organisations are perennial problems that warrant further rigorous investigation. However, the former problems are currently incompatible with doctoral research for several reasons. Firstly, the expected duration of a doctorate is insufficient. Secondly, these topics characteristically require multidisciplinary approaches, whereas doctorates are typically disciplinary-based. Straddling disciplinary boundaries adds theoretical and methodological complications to an already challenging qualification. Thirdly, to provide workable solutions the research needs translation. This requires an ecosystem that supports this translation, but this may not exist. These currently make substantial practical and policy impact from doctoral research infeasible. Nevertheless, this should not divert our attention and energy away from these important issues.

Final observation

This manifesto for impact of doctoral programmes brings to the fore consideration and concern for the people involved in the relationship between the student and the supervisor which lies at the heart of doctoral education. While this may be a surprise, it should not be. The UK QAA doctoral descriptor (Box 7.1) outlines the skills an individual should have acquired on completion of the degree. The League of European Research Universities (LERU) note that research training should produce "creative, critical, autonomous, intellectual risk takers" (LERU, 2010: 3). And doctoral supervisors consider the core purpose of a doctorate is the development of the person (Åkerlind & McAlpine, 2017). Somehow this focus on the person has been lost in the commodification of research outputs. Instead, we need to recognise and value the contribution that highly trained individuals can make to their organisations and wider society. This is the path to genuine sustainable research impact from doctoral research.

Points to ponder

1 Does doctoral research in Business and Management have genuine scholarly or practical and policy impact?
2 How might the development of an individual be assessed in a *viva voce*?
3 How can doctoral programmes be designed to address societal issues?

References

Amundsen, C., and McAlpine, L. (2009). 'Learning supervision': trial by fire. *Innovation in Education and Teaching International*, 46 (3), 331–342.

Åkerlind, G. (2008). Growing and developing as a university researcher. *Higher Education*, 55 (2), 241–254.

Åkerlind, G., and McAlpine, L. (2017). Supervising doctoral students: variation in purpose and pedagogy. *Studies in Higher Education*, 42 (9), 1686–1698.

Ali, P.A., Watson, R., and Dhingra, K. (2016). Postgraduate research students' and their supervisors' attitudes towards supervision. *International Journal of Doctoral Studies*, 11, 227–241.

Alvesson, M., Ashcroft, K., and Thomas, R. (2008). Identity matters: reflections on the construction of identity scholarships in organization studies. *Organization*, 15 (1), 5–28.

Archer, L. (2008). Younger academics' constructions of authenticity, success and professional identity. *Studies in Higher Education*, 33 (4), 385–403.

Armsby, P., Costley, C., and Cranfield, S. (2018). The design of doctorate curricula for practising professionals. *Studies in Higher Education*, 43 (12), 2226–2237.

Ashkanasy, N.M. (2011). Advancing theory: more than just 'gap filling'. *Journal of Organizational Behavior*, 32, 819–821.

Baker, M., and Bourne, M. (2014). A governance framework for the idea-to-launch process: development and application of a governance framework for new product development. *Research Technology Management*, 57 (1), 42–48.

Bandola-Gill, J., and Smith, K.E. (2022). Governing by narratives: REF impact case studies and restrictive storytelling in performance. *Studies in Higher Education*, 47 (9), 1857–1871.

Banerjee, S., and Morley, C. (2013). Professional doctorates in management: toward a practice-based approach to doctoral education. *Academy of Management Learning and Education*, 12, 173–193.

Baptista, A., Frick, L., Holley, K., Remmik, M., Tesch, J., and Åkerlind, G. (2015). The doctorate as an original contribution to knowledge: considering relationships between originality, creativity and innovation. *Frontline Learning Research*, 3 (3), 55–67.

Bareham, J., Bourner, T., and Stevens, G.R. (2000). The DBA: what is it for? *Career Development International*, 5 (7), 394–403.

Barnes, B.J., and Austin, A.E. (2009). The role of doctoral advisors: a look at advising from the advisor's perspective. *Innovative High Education*, 33, 297–315.

Bartunek, J.M., and Rynes, S.L. (2014). Academics and practitioners are alike and unlike: the paradoxes of academic-practitioner relationships. *Journal of Management*, 40, 1181–1201.

Bastalich, W. (2017). Content and context in knowledge production: a critical review of doctoral supervision literature. *Studies in Higher Education*, 42 (7), 1145–1157.

Bastow, S., Dunleavy, P., and Tinkler, J. (2014). *The impact of social sciences: how academics and their research make a difference*. London: SAGE Publications Ltd.

Beauchamp, C., Jazvac-Martek, M., and McAlpine, L. (2009). Studying doctoral education: using activity theory to shape methdological tools. *Innovations in Education and Teaching International*, 46, 265–277.

Becher, T., and Trowler, P.R. (2001). *Academic tribes and territories*. Buckingham: Open University Press.

Beech, N. (2011). Liminality and the practices of identity reconstruction. *Human Relations*, 64, 285–302.

Boehe, D.M. (2016). Supervisory styles: a contingency framework. *Studies in Higher Education*, 41 (3), 399–414.

Boman, J., Beeson, H., Sanchez Barrioluengo, M., and Rusitoru, M. (2021). *What comes after a PhD? Findings from the DocEnhance survey of doctorate holders on their employment situation, skills match and the value of the doctorate*. European Science Foundation (ESF). https://docenhance.eu/wordpress/wp-content/uploads/2021/12/DocEnhance-D1.2_Report-on-career-tracking-of-PhD-graduates.pdf

Bourner, T. (2016). A guide to professional doctorates in business and management. *Action Learning: Research and Practice*, 13, 294–298.

Bourner, T., Bowden, R., and Laing, S. (2001). Professional doctorates in England. *Studies in Higher Education*, 26 (1), 65–83.

Brailsford, I. (2010). Motives and aspirations for doctoral study: careers, personal and inter-personal factors in the decision to embark on a History PhD. *International Journal of Doctoral Studies*, 5, 15–27.

Brammer, S.J., Branicki, L., Linnenluecke, M.K., and Smith, T. (2019). Grand challenges in management research: attributes, achievements, and advancement. *Australian Journal of Management*, 44, 517–533.

Briner, R.B., Denyer, D., and Rousseau, D.M. (2009). Evidence-based management: concept-clean-up time? *Academy of Management Perspectives*, 23 (4), 19–32.

British Academy (2021). *Business and management provision in UK higher education*. https://www.thebritishacademy.ac.uk/publications/business-and-management-provision-in-uk-higher-education/ (accessed 10 October 2023).

Brown, A. (2017). Identity work and organizational identification. *International Journal of Management Reviews*, 19, 296–317.

Brown, A.D. (2015). Identities and identity work in organizations. *International Journal of Management Reviews*, 17, 20–40.

Bryan, B., and Guccione, K. (2018). Was it worth it? A qualitative exploration into graduate perceptions of doctoral value. *Higher Education Research and Development*, 37 (6), 1124–1140.

Burgess, H., Weller, G., and Wellington, J. (2013). The connection between professional doctorates and the workplace: symbiotic relationship or loose association. *Work-Based Learning E-Journal International*, 3 (1), 1.

Burgess, H., and Wellington, J. (2010). Exploring the impact of professional doctorates on students' professional practice and personal development. Early indications. *Work-Based Learning E-Journal*, 1 (1), 160–176.

Casey, B.H. (2009). The economic contribution of PhDs. *Journal of Higher Education Policy and Management*, 31 (3), 219–227.

Coffman, K., Putman, P., Adkisson, A., Kriner, B., and Monaghan, C. (2016). Waiting for the expert to arrive: using a community of practice to develop the scholarly identity of doctoral students. *International Journal of Teaching and Learning in Higher Education, 28* (1), 30–37.

Cornell, B. (2020). *PhD students and their careers*. Higher Education Policy Institute, Policy.

Cotterall, S. (2015). The rich get richer: international doctoral candidates and scholarly identity. *Innovations in Education and Teaching International*, 52 (4), 360–370.

Couston, A., and Pignatel, I. (2018). PhDs in business: nonsense, or opportunity or both? *Global Business and Organizational Excellence*, 37 (2), 49–58.

Creaton, J., and Anderson, V. (2021). The impact of the professional doctorate on managers' professional practice. *International Journal of Management Education*, 19, 100461.

De Grande, H., De Boyser, K., Vandevelde, K., and Van Rossem, R. (2014). From academia to industry: are doctorate holders ready? *Journal of the Knowledge Economy*, 5, 538–561.

Denicolo, P.M., and Park, C. (2013). Doctorateness – an elusive concept? In M. Kompf and P.M. Denicolo (Eds) *Critical issues in higher education* (pp. 191–197). Rotterdam: SensePublishers.

Deuchar, R. (2008). Facilitator, director or critical friend?: contradiction and congruence in doctoral supervision styles. *Teaching in Higher Education*, 13 (4), 489–500.

Diamond, A., Ball, C., Vorley, T., Highes, T., Moreton, R., and Nathwani, T. (2014). *The impact of doctoral careers*. Leicester: CFE Research.

Dos Santos, L.M., and Fai Lo, H. (2018). The development of doctoral degree curriculum in England: perspectives from professional doctoral degree graduates. *International Journal of Education Policy & Leadership*, 23 (6), 1–19.

East, L., Stokes, R., and Walker, M. (2014). Universities, the public good and professional education in the UK. *Studies in Higher Education*, 39 (9), 1617–1633.

Economic and Social Research Council (2021a). *Review of the PhD in the social sciences*. https://www.ukri.org/wp-content/uploads/2022/03/ESRC-020322-Review-of-the-PhD-in-the-Social-Sciences.pdf (accessed 22 July 2023).

Economic and Social Research Council (2021b). *Review of the PhD in the social sciences: ESRC response*. Leicester: CFE Research.

Economic and Social Research Council (2023). *Defining impact*. https://www.ukri.org/councils/esrc/impact-toolkit-for-economic-and-social-sciences/defining-impact/ (accessed 10 October 2023).

ESRC (2005). *Postgraduate training guidelines*. Swindon: ESRC.

ESRC (2022). *Strengthening the role of training needs analysis in doctoral training*. Swindon: UKRI.

EUA (2005). Bologna Seminar on "Doctoral Programmes for the European Knowledge Society." *Conclusions and Recommendations*. Salzburg 3–5 February 2005.

EUA (2022). *Building the foundations of research. A vision for the future of doctoral education in Europe*. Geneva, Switzerland: EUA-CDA.

Feng Teng, M. (2020). A narrative enquiry of identity construction in academic communities of practice: voices from a Chinese doctoral student in Hong Kong. *Pedagogies: An International Journal*, 15 (1), https://doi.org/10.1080/1554480X.2019.1673164.

Fenge, L.A. (2008). Professional doctorates – a better route for researching professionals? *Social Work in Education*, 28, 165–176.

Fenge, L.A. (2012). Enhancing the doctoral journey: the role of group supervision in supporting collaborative learning and creativity. *Studies in Higher Education*, 37 (4), 401–414.

Gatfield, T. (2005). An investigation into PhD supervisory management styles: development of a dynamic conceptual model and its managerial implications. *Journal of Higher Education Policy and Management*, 27 (3), 311–325.

George, G., Howard-Grenville, J., Joshi, J., and Tihanyi, L. (2016). Understanding and tackling societal grand challenges through management research. *Academy of Management Journal*, 59 (6), 1880–1895.

Ghoshal, S. (2005). Bad management theories are destroying good management practices. *Academy of Management Learning & Education*, 4 (1), 75–91.

Gibbons, M.C., Limoges, H., Nowotny, S., Schwartzman, S., Scott, P., and Trow, M. (1994). *The new production of knowledge: the dynamics of science and research in contemporary societies*. London: SAGE.

González-Ocampo, G., and Castelló, M. (2019). Supervisors were first students: analysing supervisors' perceptions as doctoral students versus doctoral supervisors. *Innovations in Education and Teaching International*, 56 (6), 711–725.

Green, B. (2005). Unfinished business: subjectivity and supervision. Higher Education Research & Development, 24, 151–163.

Guerin, C., and Green, I. (2015). 'They're the bosses': feedback in team supervision. *Journal of Further and Higher Education*, 39 (3), 320–335.

Guerin, C., Kerr, H., and Green, I. (2015). Supervision pedagogies: narratives from the field. *Teaching in Higher Education*, 20 (1), 107–118.

Halse, C., and Malfroy, J. (2010). Retheorizing doctoral supervision as professional work. *Studies in Higher Education*, 35 (1), 79–92.

Halse, C., and Mowbray, S. (2011). The impact of the doctorate. *Studies in Higher Education*, 36(5), 513–525.

Hambrick, D.C. (1994). What if the academy actually mattered? *Academy of Management Review*, 19 (1), 11–16.

Hancock, S. (2021). What is known about doctoral employment? Reflections from a UK study and directions for future research. *Journal of Higher Education Policy and Management*, 43 (5), 520–536.

Hanson, S. (2020). *The employment of PhD graduates in the UK: what do we know?* HEPI. https://www.hepi.ac.uk/2020/02/17/the-employment-of-phd-graduates-in-the-uk-what-do-we-know/ (accessed 22 July 2023).

Hasgall, A., and Peneoasu, A.-M. (2022). *Doctoral education in Europe: current developments and trends*. Geneva, Switzerland: European University Association Council for Doctoral Education.

Hawkins, B., and Edwards, G. (2015). Managing the monsters of doubt: liminality, threshold concepts and leadership learning. *Management Learning*, 46 (1), 24–43.

Hay, A. (2014). "I don't know what I am doing!": surfacing struggles of managerial identity work. *Management Learning*, 45 (5), 509–524.

Hay, A., and Hodgkinson, M. (2008). More success than meets the eye – a challenge to critiques of the MBA. *Management Learning*, 39 (1), 21–40.

Hay, A., and Samra-Fredericks, D. (2016). Desperately seeking fixedness: practitioners' accounts of 'becoming doctoral researchers'. *Management Learning*, 47 (4), 407–423.

Hay, A., and Samra-Fredericks, D. (2019). Bringing the heart and soul back in: collaborative inquiry and the DBA. *Academy of Management Learning and Education*, 18 (1), 59–80.

HEFCE (2019). *REF2021 Panel criteria and working methods*. Bristol: HEFCE.

Hemer, S.R. (2012). Informality, power and relationships in postgraduate supervision: supervising PhD candidates over coffee. *Higher Education Research & Development*, 31 (6), 827–839.

HESA (2023). *Who's studying in HE?* https://www.hesa.ac.uk/data-and-analysis/students/whos-in-he (accessed 10 October 2023).

Hnatkova, E., Degtyarova, I., Kersschot, M., and Boman, J. (2022). Labour market perspectives for PhD graduates in Europe. *European Journal of Education*, 57, 395–409.

House of Commons Science and Technology Committee (2013). *Bridging the valley of death: improving the commercialisation of research*. https://publications.parliament.uk/pa/cm201213/cmselect/cmsctech/348/348.pdf (accessed 18 October 2023).

Hughes, T., Webber, D., and O'Regan, N. (2019). Achieving wider impact in business and management: analysing the case studies from REF 2014. *Studies in Higher Education*, 44 (4), 628–642.

Ibarra, H. (2003). *Working Identity: unconventional strategies for reinventing your career*. Boston, MA: Harvard Business School Press.

IFSAM (2021). *IFSAM General Assembly's position statement on management research*. International Federation of Scholarly Associations of Management, Brussels, Belgium. https://www.ifsam.org/ifsam-soft-policy-statements/ (accessed 11 October 2023).

Janta, H., Lugosi, P., and Brown, L. (2014). Coping with loneliness: a netnographic study of doctoral students. *Journal of Further and Higher Education*, 38 (4), 553–571.

Johansson, C., and Yerrabati, S. (2017). A review of the literature on professional doctorate supervisory styles. *Management in Education*, 31 (4), 166–171.

Jones, M. (2018). Contemporary trends in professional doctorates. *Studies in Higher Education*, 43 (5), 814–825.

Kasworm, C. (2010). Adult learners in a research university: negotiating undergraduate student identity. *Adult Education Quarterly*, 60 (2), 143–160.

Kearns, H., Gardiner, M., and Marshall, K. (2008). Innovation in PhD completion: the hardy shall succeed (and be happy!). *Higher Education Research and Development*, 27 (1), 77–89.

Kehm, B.M. (2004). Developing doctoral degrees and qualifications in Europe: good practice and issues of concern – a comparative analysis. In J. Sadlak (Ed) *Doctoral studies and qualifications in Europe and the United States: status and prospects* (pp. 279–298). Bucharest: UNESCO-CEPES.

Kempster, S. (2009). *How managers have learnt to lead: exploring the development of leadership practice*. Basingstoke: Palgrave-Macmillan.

Kets de Vries, M., and Korotov, K. (2007). Creating transformational executive education programs. *Academy of Management Learning and Education*, 6, 375–387.

Kirchherr, J. (2018). A PhD should be about improving society not chasing academic kudos. *The Guardian*, 9 August.

Kot, F.C., and Hendel, D.D. (2012). Emergence and growth of professional doctorates in the United States, United Kingdom, Canada and Australia: a comparative analysis. *Studies in Higher Education*, 37 (3), 345–364.

Kunisch, S., zu Knyphausen-Aufsess, D., Bapuji, H., Aguinis, H., Bansal, T., Tsui, A., and Pinto, J. (2023). Using review articles to address societal grand challenges. *International Journal of Management Reviews*, 25, 240–250.

Lambert, R. (2003). *Lambert review of business-university collaboration*. Final report. London: HM Treasury.

Lariviere, V. (2012). On the shoulders of students? The contribution of PhD students to the advancement of knowledge. *Scientometrics*, 90, 463–481.

Larivière, V. (2013). PhD students' excellence scholarships and their relationship with research productivity, scientific impact and degree completion. *Canadian Journal of Higher Education*, 43 (2), 27–41.

Lave, J., and Wenger, E. (1991). *Situated learning: legitimate peripheral participation*. Cambridge: Cambridge University Press.

Lee, A. (2008). How are doctoral students supervised? Concepts of doctoral research supervision. *Studies in Higher Education*, 33 (3), 267–281.

Leitch, S. (2006). *Leitch review of skills: prosperity for all in the global economy – world class skills*. Norwich: Her Majesty's Stationary Office.

LERU (2010). *Doctoral degrees beyond 2010: training talented researchers for society*. Leuven, Belgium: LERU.

LERU (2014). *Good practices elements in doctoral training*. Advice Paper 15. Leuven, Belgium: LERU.

Liedtka, J. (2013). *Design thinking: what it is and why it works*. Design at Darden Working Paper Series.

Lovitts, B.E. (2005). Being a good course taker is not enough: a theoretical perspective on the transition to independent research. *Studies in Higher Education*, 39 (2), 137–154.

MacIntosh, R., Mason, K., Beech, N., and Bartunek, J.M. (2021). *Delivering impact in management research, when does it really happen?* London and New York: Routledge.

Mantai, L. (2017). Feeling like a resarcher: experiences of early doctoral students in Australia. *Studies in Higher Education*, 42 (4), 636–650.

Marcos, J., and Denyer, D. (2012). Crossing the sea from they to we? The unfolding of knowing and practising in collaborative research. *Management Learning*, 43 (4), 443–459.

McAlpine, L., and Amundsen, C. (2009). Identity and agency: pleasures and collegiality among the challenges of the doctoral journey. *Studies in Continuing Education*, 31 (2), 109–125.

McAlpine, L., and Inouye, K. (2022). What value do PhD graduates offer? An organizational case study. *Higher Education Research & Development*, 41 (5), 1648–1663.

McAlpine, L., and McKinnon, M. (2013). Supervision – the most variable of variables: student perspectives. *Studies in Continuing Education*, 35 (3), 265–280.

McAlpine, L., and Norton, J. (2006). Reframing our approach to doctoral programs: an integrative framework for action and research. *Higher Education Research & Development*, 25 (1), 3–17.

Miller, D. (2007). Paradigm prison, or in praise of atheoretic research. *Strategic Organization*, 5 (2), 177–184.

Mowbray, S., and Halse, C. (2010). The purpose of the PhD: theorising the skills acquired by students. *Higher Education Research & Development*, 29 (6), 653–664.

Murphy, N., Bain, J.D., and Conrad, L. (2007). Orientations to research higher degree supervision. *Higher Education*, 53, 209–234.

Murray, R., and Cunningham, E. (2011). Managing researcher development: 'drastic transition'? *Studies in Higher Education*, 36, 831–845.

Nasiri, F., and Mafakheri, F. (2015). Postgraduate research supervision at a distance: a review of challenges and strategies. *Studies in Higher Education*, 40 (10), 1962–1969.

Nature (2019). The mental health of PhD researchers demands urgent attention. *Nature*, 575, 257–258.

Nerad, M. (2004). The PhD in the US: criticisms, facts and remedies. *Higher Education Policy*, 17, 183–199.

Neumann, R. (2005). Doctoral differences: professional doctorates and PhDs compared. *Journal of Higher Education Policy and Management*, 27, 173–188.

Nulty, D., Kiley, M., and Meyers, N. (2009). Promoting and recognising excellence in the supervision of research students: an evidence-based framework. *Assessment & Evaluation in Higher Education*, 34 (6), 693–707.

Nyquist, J.D., and Woodford, B.J. (2000). *Re-envisioning the PhD: what concerns do we have?* Seattle: University of Washington.

Overall, N.C., Deane, K.L., and Peterson, E.R. (2011). Promoting doctoral students' research self efficacy: combining academic guidance with autonomy support. *Higher Education Research & Development*, 30 (6), 791–805.

Park, C. (2005). New variant PhD: the changing nature of the doctorate in the UK. *Journal of Higher Education Policy and Management*, 27 (2), 189–207.

Parry, E., and Ryals, L. (2014). Student experience and student progress through a professional doctorate: a longitudinal study. *Paper presented at UKGCE Conference*, Cardiff, 2014.

Patterson, C.A., Chang, C.N., Lavadia, C.N., Pardo, M.L., Fowler, D.A., and Butler-Purry, K. (2019). Transforming doctoral education: preparing multidimensional and adaptive scholars. *Studies in Graduate and Postdoctoral Education*, 11 (1), 17–34, https://doi.org/10.1108/SGPE-03-2019-0029.

Pedersen, H.S. (2014). New doctoral graduates in the knowledge economy: trends and key issues. *Journal of Higher Education Policy and Management*, 36 (6), 632–645.

Petriglieri, G.P., and Petriglieri, J.L. (2010). Identity work spaces: the case of business schools. *Academy of Management Learning and Education*, 9 (1), 44–60.

Pettigrew, A.M. (1997). The double hurdles for management research. In T. Clarke (Ed) *Advancement in organizational behaviour: essays in honour of J.S. Pugh* (pp. 277–296). London: Dartmouth Press.

Philpott, C. (2015). The importance of students' motivation and identity when supervising professional doctorate students; a reflection on traditional and professional routes. *Practitioner Research in Higher Education*, 9 (1), 59–66.

Pidd, M., and Broadbent, J. (2015). Business and management studies in the 2014 Research Excellence Framework. *British Journal of Management*, 26, 569–581.

Pilbeam, C., Lloyd-Jones, G., and Denyer, D. (2012). Leveraging value in doctoral student networks through social capital. *Studies in Higher Education*, 38 (10), 1472–1489.

Poole, B. (2015). The rather elusive concept of 'doctorateness': a reaction to Wellington. *Studies in Higher Education*, 40 (9), 1507–1522.

Posselt, J. (2018). Normalizing struggle: dimensions of faculty support for doctoral students and implications for persistence and well-being. *Journal of Higher Education*, 89 (6), 988–1013.

Pyhältö, K., Vekkaila, J., and Keskinen, J. (2015). Fit matters in the supervisory relationship: doctoral students and supervisors perceptions about the supervisory activities. *Innovations in Education and Teaching International*, 52 (1), 4–16.

Quality Assurance Agency (2014). *UK quality code for higher education. Part A: setting and maintaining academic standards*. https://www.qaa.ac.uk/docs/qaa/quality-code/qualifications-frameworks.pdf (accessed 27 October 2023).

Quality Assurance Agency (2018). *UK quality code for higher education. Advice and guidance. Research degrees*. Gloucester: The Quality Assurance Agency for Higher Education.

Riva, E., Gracia, L., and Limb, R. (2022). Using co-creation to facilitate PhD supervisory relationships. *Journal of Further and Higher Education*, 46(7), 913–930.

Roberts, G. (2002). *Set for success: the supply of people with science, technology, engineering and mathematics skills*. London: HM Treasury.

Robertson, M.J. (2017). Team modes and power: supervision of doctoral students. *Higher Education Research & Development*, 36 (2), 358–371.

Sainsbury, L. (2007). *The race to the top: a review of government's science and innovation policies*. London: HMSO.

Salipante, P., and Smith, A.K. (2012). From the 3 Rs to the 4 Rs: toward doctoral education that encourages evidence-based management through problem-solving research. In D. Rousseau (Ed) *Oxford handbook of evidence-based management* (pp. 356–376). Oxford: Oxford University Press.

Sambrook, S., and Stewart, J. (2008). Developing critical reflection in professional focused doctorates: a facilitator's perspective. Journal of European Industrial Training, 32 (5), 359–373.

Seelos, C., Mair, J., and Traeger, C. (2023). The future of grand challenges research: retiring a hopeful concept and endorsing research principles. *International Journal of Management Research*, 25, 251–269.

Sharma, G., and Bansal, P. (2020). Cocreating rigorous and relevant knowledge. *Academy of Management Journal*, 63 (2), 386–410.

Simpson, C., and Sommer, D. (2016). The practice of professional doctorates. *Journal of Management Education*, 40, 576–594.

Skakni, I., Inouye, K., and McAlpine, L. (2022). PhD holders entering non-academic workplaces: organisational culture shock. *Studies in Higher Education*, 47 (6), 1271–1283.

Smith, A. (2010). *One step beyond: making the most of postgraduate education*. https://dera.ioe.ac.uk/id/eprint/470/7/10-704-one-step-beyond-postgraduate-education_Redacted.pdf (accessed 9 December 2023).

Stern, L.N. (2016). *Building on success and learning from experience: an independent review of the research excellence framework*. https://assets.publishing.service.gov.uk/media/5a803df4e5274a2e8ab4f03d/ind-16-9-ref-stern-review.pdf (accessed 10 October 2023).

Sturdy, A., Brocklehurst, M., Winstanley, D., and Littlejohns, M. (2006). Management as a (self) confidence trick: management ideas, education and identity work. *Organization*, 13 (6), 841–860.

Taylor, R.T., Vitale, T., Tapoler, C., and Whaley, K. (2018). Desirable qualities of modern doctorate advisors in the USA: a view through the lenses of candidates, graduates, and academic advisors. *Studies in Higher Education*, 43 (5), 854–866.

Taylor, S. (2022). *Developments in the doctoral examination in the UK*. Litchfield: UKCGE.

Tenkasi, R. (2011). Integrating theory to inform practice: insights from the practitioner–scholar. In S.A. Mohrman and E.E. Lawler (Eds) *Useful research: advancing theory and practice* (pp. 211–232). San Francisco, CA: Berrett Koehler.

Tranfield, D., and Starkey, K. (1998). The nature, social organization and promotion of management research: towards policy. *British Journal of Management*, 9, 341–353.

UKCGE (2021). *UK research supervision survey 2021 report*. Litchfield: UKCGE.

Urbina-Garcia, A. (2020). What do we know about university academics' mental health? A systematic literature review. *Stress and Health*, 36, 563–585.

Usher, R. (2002). A diversity of doctorates: fitness for the knowledge economy? *Higher Education Research & Development*, 21 (2), 143–153.

Van Aken, J.E. (2005). Management research as a design science: articulating the research products of mode 2 knowledge production in management. *British Journal of Management*, 16, 19–36.

Van Gennep, A. (1960). *The rites of passage*. Chicago, IL: University of Chicago Press.

Vitae (2011). *The researcher development framework*. https://www.vitae.ac.uk/researchers-professional-development/about-the-vitae-researcher-development-framework

Warry, P. (2006). *Increasing the economic impact of the research councils*. London: Research Council Economic Impact Group.

Watermeyer, R. (2016). Impact in the REF: issues and obstacles. *Studies in Higher Education*, 41 (2), 199–214.

Watermeyer, R., and Hedgecoe, A. (2016). Selling 'impact': peer reviewer projections of what is needed and what counts in REF impact case studies. A retrospective analysis. *Journal of Education Policy*, 31 (5), 651–665.

Wellington, J. (2013). Searching for 'doctorateness'. *Studies in Higher Education*, 38 (10), 1490–1503.

Wellington, J., and Sikes, P. (2006). A doctorate in a tight compartment: why do students choose a professional doctorate and what impact does it have on their personal and professional lives? *Studies in Higher Education*, 31 (6), 723–734.

Whetten, D.A. (1989). What constitutes a theoretical contribution? *Academy of Management Review*, 14 (4), 490–495.

Wiegerová, A. (2016). A study of the motives of doctoral students. *Procedia – Social and Behavioral Sciences*, 217, 123–131.

Wisker, G., and Robinson, G. (2012). Picking up the pieces: supervisors and doctoral "orphans". *International Journal for Researcher Development*, 3 (2), 139–153.

Wright, A., Murray, J.P., and Geale, P. (2007). A phenomenographic study of what it means to supervise doctoral students. *Academy of Management Learning & Education*, 6 (4), 458–474.

Yazdani, S., and Shokooh, F. (2018). Defining doctorateness: a concept analysis. *International Journal of Doctoral Studies*, 13, 31–48.

Index

Note: **Bold** page numbers refer to tables; *italic* page numbers refer to figures.

Simpson, C. 41
skills development/skills training 33, 45,
    51, 58, 59, 63–65
skills requirement 63–65
Smith, K.E. 23
Sommer, D. 41
standards 13–15, 19, 60, 61
Stern, L. N. 3
study full-time (FT) students 55, 60, 64–65
study part-time (PT) students 55, 60,
    61, 65
supervision 49, 65; challenges of
    54–56; doctoral programmes 73–74;
    high-quality 16; nature and type of
    49–51
supervisor(s) 16, 17, 26, 45, 50, 73; role
    49, 51–54, **52**, *53,* **54,** 73
supervisory training 56–57
Supportive Guide 51, **52**
sustainable development goals (SDGs)
    6, 69, 74

teaching 13, 34, 38, 44, 58, 71
team supervision 50
3P's framework 7, 66; *see also* person;
    process; product
traditional master-apprentice model 50
Trafford and Leshem's model 14
training 27, 49, 59; in research methods
    15, 18, 24, 38, 61, 71, 73, 74; skills
    requirement and 63–65; supervisory
    56–57; transferable skills 34
training needs analysis (TNA) 64
transferable skills 27, 34–36, 38, 64, 73
transition, identity 40, 41, 43, 44–45

UK: -based DBA 19, 22, 32, 62, 69;
    doctoral examinations in 14, 61;
    doctoral graduates in 71; doctoral
    programmes in 1, 5, 11, 64,
    68; doctoral supervisors in 55;
    funding for FT students 60; higher
    education institutions 1, 17, 20,
    69; national assessment exercises
    23; PhD in 4, 18, 34; policy
    guidance 58; research councils 70;
    research evaluation in 3; Research
    Excellence Framework process
    3, 20, 22, 23, 25, 28, 58, 69;
    universities 1, 15, 25, 28
UK Government House of Commons
    Science and Technology Committee
    55–56
USA: DBA programme in 44, 69; PhD in
    4, 18, 34, 71
Usher, R. 15

value 34, 53, 71; impact on policy and
    practice 25–26; of scholarly impact
    16–18
Vitae Researcher Development
    Framework 38, 58, 64
viva voce 14, 73

Wellington, J. 14
Wenger, E. 40, 50
Wisker, G. 50
Woodford, B.J. 18
Wright, A. 51, 57

Yazdani, S. 13, 33

For Product Safety Concerns and Information please contact our EU
representative GPSR@taylorandfrancis.com
Taylor & Francis Verlag GmbH, Kaufingerstraße 24, 80331 München, Germany